To Dr. Jake Schrum —

I hope you'll find this new perspective on higher education to be both interesting, and useful —

Best —

Phil

Reconstructing Alma Mater:
The Coming Crisis in Higher Education

A Blueprint for Reform

Reconstructing Alma Mater: The Coming Crisis in Higher Education

A Blueprint for Reform

Philip H. Francis

Algora Publishing
New York

© 2006 by Algora Publishing.
All Rights Reserved
www.algora.com

No portion of this book (beyond what is permitted by
Sections 107 or 108 of the United States Copyright Act of 1976)
may be reproduced by any process, stored in a retrieval system,
or transmitted in any form, or by any means, without the
express written permission of the publisher.
ISBN: 0-87586-458-9 (trade soft)
ISBN: 0-87586-459-7 (hard cover)
ISBN: 0-87586-460-0 (ebook)

Library of Congress Cataloging-in-Publication Data —

Francis, Philip H.

Reconstructing Alma Mater : the coming crisis in higher education, a blueprint for reform / Philip H. Francis.

p. cm.

ISBN 0-87586-458-9 (trade paper : alk. paper) — ISBN 0-87586-459-7 (hard cover : alk. paper) — ISBN 0-87586-460-0 (ebook) 1. Education, Higher—United States—Forecasting. 2. Education, Higher—Economic aspects—United States. I. Title.

LA227.4.F89 2006

378.73—dc22

2006005018

Front Cover: Columbia University Commencement Exercises. Columbia University's Alma Mater statue during Columbia 2005 commencement ceremony. Columbia will graduate approximately 11,000 students from all schools marking Columbia University's 251st academic year.
Image: © James Leynse/Corbis
Photographer: James Leynse Date Photographed: May 18, 2005

Printed in the United States

This book is dedicated to all those in the higher academic community: presidents and chancellors, deans, faculty and administrative staff. Additionally, we salute each generation of students, for they are our best bet for a better future.

Table of Contents

Prologue	1
Chapter I: The Beginnings and the Journey	3
1. The Audience and the Message	3
Finance	6
Demographics	6
Technology	7
Competition	7
Marketplace	7
Politics	7
2. About this Book	7
Chapter II: Laying the Foundation for Tomorrow's Higher Education Systems	13
1. A Short History of the Structure of Colleges and Universities	13
2. Government's Early Role in Proliferating Higher Education: A Briefing	19
3. The Distinctive and Changing Culture of the Modern University	21
4. Creating Knowledge Workers	31
Chapter III: Beginnings of the New Transformation	35
Process, Process, Process	35
1. The Input Side: K-12 Education	35
2. Accreditation of Colleges and Universities	44
3. The Structure of Colleges and Universities	46
4. Admissions: Gatekeepers, Diversity and Affirmative Action	50
5. The Learning Environment	59
6. Pedagogy: Trends and Measuring Educational Outcomes	75

CHAPTER IV: TECHNOLOGY'S TRANSFORMATIONAL ROLE IN
HIGHER EDUCATION
- SYSTEMS THAT ARE NEEDED TO TAKE US INTO THE FUTURE 79
  1. FORCES OF CHANGE: DEMOGRAPHICS AND ACCELERATING KNOWLEDGE 79
  2. TECHNOLOGY: CONVENTIONAL, DISTANCE AND INTERNET-BASED LEARNING 85
  3. BUSINESS INFORMATION & LIBRARY SYSTEMS 97
  4. MANAGING AND REINING IN TECHNOLOGY COSTS 104
  5. INSTITUTIONAL IT POLICY 108
  6. BENCHMARKING 112
  7. LIBRARIES 114

CHAPTER V: THE NEW BUSINESS OF HIGHER EDUCATION
- THE NEW BUSINESS OF HIGHER EDUCATION 117
  1. CORE ACADEMIC VALUES: LEADERSHIP, ACADEMIC POLICY, ETHICS, BRANDING 117
     - Leadership 118
     - Academic Policy 122
     - Ethics: Cheating and Honor Codes 126
     - Branding 128
  2. UNIVERSITIES EMULATING BUSINESS 131
     1. Lack of Urgency 133
     2. Limited Staff Engagement 133
     3. Imbedded Culture 134
     4. Value 134
     5. Management Perspective 134
  3. THE COST STRUCTURE AND ECONOMICS OF HIGHER EDUCATION 149
     - Endowments and Business Planning 152
     - Entrepreneurship 155
     - Trends to Watch 165
     - Faculty and Staff 167
  4. TENURE AND COLLECTIVE BARGAINING 172
  5. THE WORKFORCE OF THE FUTURE: KNOWLEDGE 184

CHAPTER VI: GETTING THE MOST, WHILE MANAGING COSTS 187
  1. TEACHING AND LEARNING: ARE STUDENTS GETTING WHAT THEY NEED? 187
  2. COLLEGE ATHLETICS AND RECREATION 190
  3. PHONY DEGREES: NEW TWISTS ON EDUCATION AND MEASURING EDUCATIONAL OUTCOMES 196
  4. LEARNING BY DEGREES 198

EPILOGUE 201

Prologue

Everything that is known had a beginning somewhere, sometime. Scholars say that the "big bang" birthed the universe, perhaps multiple universes. But it will never be known nor can it even be imagined what was before that glorious instant. It was the beginning.

On a more familiar scale, all the rivers and oceans had a time and place where they began, before which they did not exist. The great Mississippi River began near the end of the most recent Ice Age, more than 10,000 years ago. The river begins at spring-fed Lake Itasca, in a northern Minnesota swampland, then becomes ever more mighty as it courses southward toward the Gulf of Mexico, gathering from many other river sources—which likewise had their own beginnings. And America's native peoples, living along this giant river, created legends of its origins.

It is human nature to search for an understanding of the universe in order to find one's place and future—and to speculate on one's future—within it.

So it is with all beginnings. The accurate details about a particular beginning—its time and place—may not be known. But beginnings need to be imagined as benchmarks in order to understand the present and for reference points that will help to map the future. So, searches are made back in time and place that the future may be envisioned by extrapolating from past patterns. There is nothing else to go on.

And so it is with training eager minds—the focus of this book. Formal education, in the West, blossomed in the hills above Athens some

2,400 years ago, in an era of great philosophers led by Plato, Socrates and Aristotle. The Socratic Method—with the teacher posing difficult problems and students struggling to answer them—was the prototype of the modern classroom.

Plato, among the most exalted writers in all recorded history, pioneered the study of philosophy, mathematics and the natural sciences—as well as poetry, drama and architecture. He founded, and for 40 years led, the world's first learning Academy—which lasted more than 900 years, until Byzantine Emperor Justinian closed it, to purge the Academy of what he regarded as pagan practices. No other learning institution anywhere has lasted for so long.

Socrates, five years Plato's junior and regarded as the founder of Western philosophical thought, ultimately became Plato's teacher—until he, Socrates, was convicted of blasphemy and corruption of youth. He left this world on his own terms, by drinking hemlock.

And rounding off this trio of giants is Aristotle, born when Plato was at mid-life and who, more than any other thinker, determined the orientation and the content of Western intellectual history. He is held up as the first great teacher, believing that one could not claim to know a subject unless he was capable of transferring that knowledge to others. That ideal is carried on in educational centers to this very day.

This Greek trio provided the earliest Western model of intellectual instruction that is still remembered today, and an important antecedent to the modern university system. The Socratic movement in some ways was the big bang, the Mississippi, of today's educational system. In looking toward what the future holds for higher education, it is important to understand the markers that preceded us.

There is much that can be learned from history; it provides a useful, if imperfect, framework for predicting the future. Progress tends to come not as simple extensions of yesterday, but rather as discontinuous steps created by new knowledge and tools. Printing, penicillin, the automobile and the Internet come to mind as significant disruptive technologies that have changed the way people live and work. Clearly, the great innovations in information technology and their application to pedagogy and new ways of learning are just as disruptive in the field of education, and are significantly changing the way people learn.

Chapter I: The Beginnings and the Journey

Topical Themes
1. The Audience and the Message
2. About this Book

1. The Audience and the Message

This book has been written with four audiences in mind:
- Academic administrators who see opportunities in creating bold new visions of the future for their institutions.
- State and federal legislators who need to understand the financial structures and the cost-benefit relationships of public higher education.
- Academics and those aspiring to careers in higher education who want to understand what tomorrow's institution will look like.
- Entrepreneurs who are looking to the huge new markets that are being created.

The central message of this book is that higher education is on the threshold of an exciting and unprecedented transition that will bring educational transformations of immense proportions. Colleges and universities will change more in the next two decades than they have in the last two millennia. Indeed, it is already happening and rigid traditionalists of higher education who deny this watershed change are destined to be ever more marginalized—holding out on a desert island that is surrounded by a sea of educational choices and options. The challenge is, therefore, to cultivate a new breed of academic and administrative leader that will be able to mold, and capitalize upon, the possibilities of the new era; the rapid changes in demographics, lifestyles, costs, lifelong and distance learning, and even new theories about the different ways individuals learn best. And as they do so, individuals will be better prepared to manage their own futures.

The role of higher education has come under close scrutiny. Much is expected of it, yet the pressures of increasing costs and budgets, and new conceptions of its service role to society, are giving administrators many challenges. Moreover, the traditional view of colleges has been of narrowly defined, disciplined silos of scholarship. It is easy and comfortable. Yet practice has shown that it is impossible for any complex process or organization to achieve optimum performance simply by optimizing the individual pieces. This is a truth that extends to any complex organization or system, a concept which will be revisited in Chapter V.1.

Within the context of higher education, not only must administrative units be continually pushed to ever higher heights of excellence—they must also integrate to maximize synergies and achieve greater levels of educational success. Simply adding more program concentrations, internships, elective and service programs will not be sufficient. Indeed, it will take people with strong integrative and entrepreneurial skills and leadership to make this happen. These new age faculty leaders will be the agents who produce the future graduates needed.

Furthermore, this new collectivism must tackle the difficult task of finding how best to achieve genuine academic and civic engagement, how to reward these new steward-leaders. A rethink is needed on how to plan ahead in fostering collaboration and civic engagement in order to build a ore knowledgeable society. Everything should be on the table.

This is the beginning of an era of transformation in higher education. The challenge is to reconsider exactly what knowledge to deliver to future generations of students, and how to deliver it. Since medieval times, the same basic model has been used for the education of students and future leaders: they have been lectured to and tested, new knowledge has been researched and created, and young adults have been armed with the intellectual tools to carry them successfully through their lifelong careers. The process of education adopted from the beginning has generally been highly structured, standardized and somewhat inflexible. Each student has learned the same way as all others, mostly by the transference of facts and knowledge from the active professor to the passive learner. Learning has been at the feet of professors, by lectures and tests, much as in ancient times.

But the future will be significantly different in a number of ways. Modern technology provides new ways to tailor how students learn best—by blending individual inquiry with work in groups and teams, conventional teaching, and work in technology-augmented learning environments. There already is an increasing trend toward the practice of *lifelong learning*, as exemplified in part by the more than 2,000 corporate universities that provide continual education. This trend will change forever the concept of education. What then will become of the traditional student body in the 18-22 age group? It will continue to exist, but will be much different than before, as this book will demonstrate. The fact that this cohort is, today, only a small and shrinking minority of all those enrolled in higher education speaks loudly about how society will learn in the future.

Institutions will face mounting competition as their student-customers have ever greater expectations, which in turn will drive the need for better programs and greater financial controls and accountabilities. Weaker schools—especially small private liberal arts colleges—will continue to struggle for survival. Currently, they are closing at a rate of about one every two months. Institutions in general will see the need to adopt more aggressive commercial practices in branding and differentiation in order to secure and expand their market and their mind-shares. Institutional leaderships will run their organizations more like the business enterprises they are. They will be accountable for their results—the educational counterparts of the ROI and EBIT measures of the financial world. These terms may offend some, but they are even now a part of the future.

Central to this transformation are the benefits that educational technology promises. They go far beyond the familiar notions of online content accessibility, of e-learning, and the power of virtual libraries to enable rapidly the accession of tailored knowledge from world-wide sources. An analogy could be made with a small retail outlet becoming a shopping mall. The real benefit will be derived from how each student best learns as an individual. The educational equivalent of *mass customization*, which has already had enormous influence in the way the industrial sector serves its customers, will be put into practice. The learning experience, accounting for what individuals already know, and how they can best grasp and master what they do not yet know, will be tailored to each student. And the educational gains of the individual student will be measurable better than previously. Education will therefore make learning more fun, efficient and enduring than before.

So, the present higher education system is about to change considerably. There are many leading indicators to this, including:

Finance

The cost of tuition is rising at three times the cost of living. There has been a growth in staff support, from 32 administrators/1000 students twenty years ago, to 52 today. And donations of large endowments, the lack of which places many less well-off schools at a disadvantage, are increasing.

Demographics

The numbers in the traditionally considered student body of 18- to 22-year-olds are plummeting: only 16 percent of all students pursuing college work today are in this bracket. Minority, first-generation and low-income students are the fastest growing demographic. And the year 2015 will mark the beginning of a decline in the US population, following the peak of the "Boomer Progeny." In fact, for the first time in history, the world population will begin to shrink.

Technology

Simulations, virtual laboratories and online learning are transforming the way people learn. Virtual libraries are beginning to change the way they learn. And pedagogy is beginning to support tailored education and measured outcomes.

Competition

For-profit virtual universities are taking a significant market share over conventional institutions. There is a growing trend of college mergers and shared infrastructures. And the corporate university has emerged.

Marketplace

Lifelong learning is now an imperative and the need for knowledge workers overwhelms the need for traditional skills.

Politics

There is the beginning of unionism and the breakdown of the conventional tenure system, and the weakening of the cornerstone tenets of academic freedom and shared governance.

None of these developments would have been taken seriously just a decade ago. In addressing one particularly significant new movement, the *Wall Street Journal* noted that for-profit and experiential learning organizations may do to universities what health maintenance organizations have done to medicine.

2. ABOUT THIS BOOK

Many forces are converging to change forever the way higher education is viewed and practiced. To understand them and their consequences, some knowledge of the history of educational development is required. The next chapter will open with a brief summary of the evolution of the modern college/university system since the establishment of

Harvard College, America's first college, in 1636. This will lead on to the missions and cultures of the modern university. Ensuing chapters will take a close look at today's colleges and universities: their missions, cost structures, vulnerabilities, and how they dispense education. Thereafter, the cultural, economic and technological dimensions that are driving substantial changes in the educational experience of students of all ages will be examined. The basic educational foundations of academic freedom, tenure, and shared governance—and how they will be reinterpreted for the years ahead—will also be re-examined. This re-examination of the US higher educational system is the prologue to a vision of what higher education will look like in the years ahead. A compelling case will be made for a new "business model" that will lead to improved educational and institutional processes. This will then herald an era which will define the educational processes of the future.

Many of the ideas contained in this book lie outside the domain of traditional academic thought. Some of these ideas and beliefs may unsettle, perhaps even anger the reader. Although that is not the purpose, it is unequivocally true that things will not be the same. For example, it is conceded that the importance of better business models, cost accounting and management, and business strategy and processes may annoy some academics. The intention is not to be provocative, but rather to be realistic—as realistic as is possible from reading the social and economic markers already quite evident. It is also quite clear that some combination of the traditional and the newly efficient will prevail in the years ahead. Whatever else they may be, modern colleges and universities are business enterprises that will become ever more customer-centric (the students) and operate in a fiscally responsible manner within a highly segmented and competitive market space.

The author's talks and seminars with academics and educational leaders often begin with them being asked to think of themselves as the new CEO of a large, struggling company. They have to role-play as a bright, promising leader, brought in to re-energize and strengthen the company. They are eager to make their mark on their organization. They

are then asked to dig deeper and see just how huge is the challenge that confronts them. They quickly find that
- their service/product costs are rising three times faster than the consumer price index, and at double the rate of inflation;
- their administrative staff, as a percentage of their total complement, has grown by some 65 percent over the past two decades;
- their company must increasingly discount their prices in order to remain competitive;
- their company's future business depends upon expensive new technology that is costly and quickly becomes obsolete;
- most of their company's competitors are subsidized by various state and Federal funding agencies whose support is ever harder to maintain;
- their company's domestic market is forecasted to begin shrinking over the next five years, requiring increasing dependence upon foreign customers;
- their field of business is getting more crowded and competitive, and, for the first time, is being challenged by strong international players;
- and their executive team is saddled with an entrenched culture that makes it difficult, if not impossible, to make any substantive changes without protracted, often contentious, debates and studies.

They are then asked to consider how they can succeed in this environment, what their visions and strategies are. This exercise is a metaphor for the reality of today's higher educational system. The audiences usually react initially with the mantra "but we're not a business, we're educators!" Yet on closer examination, they begin to understand that higher education *is* a business. It has customers and products; it has regulated competition; and its fortunes are tightly tied to its income and balance statements. There will be those who disagree, but they should consider that over the past couple of decades, colleges and universities have continued to close their doors at unprecedented rates. The author William Arthur Ward has said, "The pessimist complains about the wind; the optimist expects it to change; and the realist adjusts the sails." It is time now to attend to the sails.

The vision developed in this book, whether it proves to be precisely or only generally correct, is intended to equip educators, legislators and trustees with the insight needed to begin moving toward a new institutional model that will be financially and competitively sound for the era ahead. Today's modern college or university is quite complex in its organization, comprising administrative and academic units that function in relative isolation from one another yet are bound together in a culture that champions ecumenism. It has outside governance for operations, and accreditation processes for quality purposes. One leading factor that makes it different from other private-sector organizations is its sources of funding, of which there are many: tuitions and stipends, legislative appropriations, capital campaigns, endowments, gifts, executive and research programs. The vast majority of higher education institutions are state-run or not-for-profit. As not-for-profits they cannot access the capital markets as for-profit enterprises do. Very often, they are strapped when it comes to funding programs and capital projects. They cannot be funded via income streams from conventional sources. These institutions may not have shareholders, but they rely heavily upon stakeholders and benefactors to make things happen over time.

The past several decades have seen the beginning of a shift from taking students for granted, to treating them as valued customers. Starting at the end of World War II, a new era was ushered in by the huge influx from the armed forces and the creation of the GI Bill. This made it possible for average Americans to go to college—in contrast to earlier years when most college students were from economically privileged families. But now, campuses had to build extra capacity to accommodate the flood of new, more mature students. There was a great expansion in community colleges, where students could get used to the challenges and discipline of higher education and, after proving themselves, could continue toward the baccalaureate degree. That boom continues. Many institutions are still overcrowded. Moreover, there has been a trend toward "branding." Institutions more and more are trying to differentiate themselves, to seek a student cohort that is less "homogenized." A particular college will be known for its student quality and for its programs in certain areas; others for athletics or social life, climate, etc. This makes it less costly to market the institution and allows it to focus on doing fewer things, but better. Each institution has its own market, and exploits it the best way it can.

These are just a few of the incremental changes that have taken place over the past half-century. But what lies ahead marginalizes, by comparison, what has already happened. In the coming chapters, the many disruptive changes ahead, and what they mean to America's higher education enterprises, will be described in detail.

But before proceeding, here are some useful Web sites for additional real-time information that may be helpful:

- International Society for Technology in Education (ISTE) — www.iste.org (see also the document http://cnets.iste.org/teachstand.html
- The Institute for Higher Education Policy — www.ihep.com (see also the document www.ihep.com/issues.html.ntls
- American Federation of Teachers (AFT) — www.aft.org (see also www.aft.org/issues/distance_ed.html
- National Education Association (NEA) — www.nea.org (see also www.nea.org/nr/nr000614.html
- American Association for Higher Education — www.aahe.org (see also www.ashe.org/bulletin/implementing%20the%seven%20prin-ciples.htm)

Chapter II: Laying the Foundation for Tomorrow's Higher Education Systems

Topical Themes
1. A Short History of the Structure of US Colleges and Universities
2. Government's Early Role in Proliferating Higher Education: a Briefing
3. The Distinctive and Changing Culture of Modern Higher Education
4. Creating Knowledge Workers

1. A Short History of the Structure of Colleges and Universities

However great and illustrious a past some institutions of learning have, the lack of real and needed change has stunted the development of many campuses. Such has been the focus on constructing buildings to meet demand that important systemic changes have been neglected. For-profits have filled the vacuum, creating competition which is good for all concerned.

America's higher education system is the world's finest. More than a third of students are enrolled in the excellent network of two-year community colleges, allowing people of all ages to develop basic skills that will enrich their lives and improve their job opportunities. The overall higher education sector is huge; five of every eight colleges and universities *in the world* are American. There are private and public; small and large; secular and denominational; civilian and military; narrowly-focused and comprehensive; prosaic and elite. There is something for everyone. And they are, collectively, the envy of the world in terms of quality, scope and depth.

It is important, however, to first have an understanding of just how American higher education earned this status. To see ahead properly, there must be an understanding of what happened in the past. The higher education system in the United States is the product of a rich legacy of struggles, starting with the Socratic era sketched briefly in Chapter I. It is the product of social revolutions, visionaries and great minds. In this chapter the development of higher education in the United States will be outlined, from its ancestry in Europe to the present day. Its current and future directions, and how they will affect the course of American competitiveness, will be discussed.

In the period between the Socratic era and the creation of the first, great universities of France, Germany and England lies a fascinating story full of secular and religious strife. The Euro-Indo Celts invaded Rome in 390 BC and soon after began to settle in what now is Ireland, and northern England. They savagely conquered the indigenous peoples along the way. In what would later be seen as the first major event in the history of Western higher education, Bishop Patrick arrived in Ireland from Rome in AD 432 with a mission to spread literacy and scholarship among the Celts and native pagans. Soon, Irish monastic schools of higher education began to spread throughout the land, welcoming clerics, commoners and noblemen alike.

In his best-selling book *How the Irish Saved Civilization*, Thomas Cahill tells us how Latin literature and heritage would almost surely have been destroyed without the Irish[1]; and how the then-illiterate Europe would not have gone on to develop its great national universities. He tells of the remarkable set of events that launched the medieval period, from the fall of Rome in AD 476, through to the Middle Ages and ending in the mid-15th century. During this period the essential characteristics of early Western higher education were formed. But the unrelenting ravages of Greek and Roman warriors of the Middle Ages put fire to all known

---

1. "How the Irish Saved Civilization," by Thomas Cahill: Anchor Books/Doubleday, 1995.

books and letters. Most of recorded Western civilization would have been lost forever, but for the holy men and women of the unconquered land that is now called Ireland. Cahill tells us that Irish monks and clerics were able to save many of the secular and religious writings and books and smuggle them out when they left Rome—teachings that surely would have perished by burning in the Roman frenzy to obliterate recorded history to that time. These anonymous clerics carefully scribed tales they had been told, which ultimately resulted in them saving the Western intellectual capital that otherwise would have been lost forever.

The beginnings of present Western higher education were formed during the period from the 11th through the 16th centuries. Higher education systems sprang up, respectively, in France, England and Germany; in the American colonies and in Russia. Although rooted in the struggles of medieval Europe, they each created their own distinctive institutions of advanced learning. These five national university models formed the basis of all modern major secular higher education systems.

The University of Paris was founded in 1170, and was the world's first great national institution of higher learning. It evolved from the cathedral schools of Notre Dame, and was composed of a faculty, students and specialized departments. Their universities operated as, and were accountable to, particular agencies of the State. Like its succeeding continental peer institutions, the University was a public institution. The French higher education system is credited with creating the model of integrating research with academic studies in order to produce scholars competent in both areas.

Soon after, in the 12th century, came Oxford which modeled itself closely on the University of Paris. (Actually, Oxford's origins go back to 1096, with scholars drawn from various orders of Roman Catholic friars.) Oxford specialized in theology and the arts, but with greater emphasis than Paris on the physical sciences. Oxford was smaller than the University of Paris and its cousin the Sorbonne, but soon developed a reputation of demanding more rigorous courses than any other of the contemporary continental universities. Cambridge was established in

1209. The English universities were largely self-governing, and were (and still are) controlled by a group of Fellows, i.e. faculty engaged in teaching or research.

Germany traces its higher education development from the year 1386, in Heidelberg. Its governance system mirrored that of both England and France in that universities were chartered and operated by the State. From the beginning, the German model saw the university as being closely tied to their various research institutes. Culturally, German students and faculty even now tend to be more nomadic than other European scholars, and have different processes for examinations and degrees than other continental countries. Its place in history is marked by the revolutionary invention of Johannes Gutenberg of movable-type printing, in the early 15th century.

The next milestone in higher education was the chartering of Harvard College in America by the General Court of the Massachusetts Bay Colony in 1636. Classes began two years later. The school was named after John Harvard, a Puritan minister who gave generously of his personal library in theology and history in order to launch the program of instruction.

The next major milestone was in 1755, when Empress Elizabeth created higher education in Russia by chartering the University of Moscow. By the end of that century, satellite universities had been created in Vilna, Kharkov, Kazan and St. Petersburg. These, and succeeding institutions, were chartered in one of three distinct categories: universities, institutes and polytechnic institutes. They continue today to have rigorous standards with highly focused curricula. Supported by government grants, their students have always been given incentives to do well; the size of the grants is keyed to individual academic progress.

What took place over these five centuries shaped the modern Western world's advanced learning systems. These medieval universities emphasized three branches of intellectualism: theology, law and "letters"—the liberal arts, including mathematics. Soon after there evolved two new distinct organizational forms of higher education. Oxford and Cambridge began to organize themselves into small, relatively autonomous colleges, sponsored and funded out of special interests by the titled and the gentry. Then, in the 16th century, the Society of Jesus began to spread colleges across Europe. This development was largely aimed at stunting the rapid growth of Protestantism. In the words of Jacques Barzun, former Provost of Columbia University, the proof of this is that nearly all great European thinkers of the following two centuries, from Descartes to Voltaire, went to Catholic Jesuit colleges, blunting the edge off new-age Christian creeds. This legacy continues in Western culture; the core of an all-purpose higher education still consists of these "arts."[2]

The emergence of America's New England colleges created a unique style of institutional governance. They were, from the beginning, exclusively private and for the privileged. Their mission was to provide training and education for the needs of a fragile nation—especially teachers, physicians and businessmen. This movement began when what are now known as the "Ivy colleges" created trustee boards composed of laymen. The idea was to democratize somewhat the governance and authority structure within the institution. But as these schools grew, this form of governance began to yield to one which gave a balance between the boards of trustees on the one hand and faculty and administrators on the other. This, for the first time in history, democratized institutional governance, the style of organization that exists today.

Up to this point there had been two major epochs in the evolution of higher education: the Greek period mentioned in Chapter I, and the early European and American periods sketched above. Both of these eras were products of disruptive social change. The Greek era launched formal education as embodied by the Socratic approach to learning. It was a unique beginning; the real start of intellectual achievement. Likewise, the launch of colleges of scholarship was credited by near-simultaneous independent advances in the early European and early American periods. It was the second "big bang."

---

2. "Trim the College? – A Utopia!" by Jacques Barzun, *The Chronicle of Higher Education*, June 22, 2001, p. B24.

The third big bang in higher education, the subject of this book, is underway. It began just after the end of World War II. Industrial productivity in the US accelerated at an annual rate of about three percent, and the American standard of living also rose steadily, year on year. But then came the mid-seventies, when it mysteriously slowed and for decades thereafter languished at closer to half that rate. As a result, the American standard of living stagnated as well. No one really knew then just why the rate of economic productivity growth took such a sharp downturn in 1973.

But something else was also changing in the mid-seventies. The American middle class family had long been composed of two employed adult members working at two paid jobs. But suddenly there began a shift in which the adult family members went from two full-time workers to just one, with the other working part time or at home. That picture now changed the typical American family. Nowadays, there are often three jobs, including the unpaid one. Time has become a more and more precious commodity. This trend is showing signs of reversal in the new millennium, in large part due to the advent of ubiquitous computers and technologies which have made it possible for us to work productively, both outside and at home. Looking ahead, it is reasonable to foresee an even more favorable future.

Society has grown accustomed to the influence of global competition for ideas and products, and for retuning itself with respect to its educational processes. Asynchronous Learning Networks (ALNs), together with high quality content and superb creative institutions, will benefit everyone in the long run. Change will come, but not overnight. For example, there are virtually no undergraduate, online engineering degrees awarded via asynchronous learning. The processes of documenting and distributing knowledge will need to be improved further. More emphasis will be placed upon the kinds of education and training needed to achieve even better productivity in the years ahead. A lot has been done over the past 30 years—but much more remains.

2. Government's Early Role in Proliferating Higher Education: a Briefing

Following the early establishment of New England's centers of higher education, and America's continued expansion westward, pressure grew to serve rural areas with practical curricula. In the latter half of the 19th century, some 80 percent of the adult population was directly linked to farming and ranching. Agriculture and veterinary sciences programs then began to appear, and the "land grant" college system was introduced. The democratization of post-secondary education was a major milestone in America's ascendancy to world prominence. Higher education was no longer only for the privileged. Men and women of ordinary means could now aspire to two-year postgraduate instruction in widening areas of practice, including home economics, journalism and engineering, and state subsidies made it affordable for them to enroll in these courses. Eastern and Midwestern states soon began to create community, or junior, colleges with the idea that students finishing such programs could then matriculate in regional or private universities for advanced studies in commerce, medicine, teaching and other fields.

This movement began with a series of Land Grants, of which the Morrill Act, signed into law by President Abraham Lincoln in 1862, was the first. It gave to each state some 30,000 acres of public land (about 50 square miles) for each state senator and representative under the 1860 census. Proceeds from the sale of these lands were to be invested in an endowment fund to support colleges of agriculture and mechanical arts for each state. The creation of the Florida Agricultural College in 1884, under the Morrill Act, gave rise to the College of Agriculture of the University of Florida in 1906. Others then followed. The Morrill Act was followed by the Hatch Act (1887) which established the Agricultural Experimental Stations in connection with these land grant institutions. Then, in 1914, the Smith-Lever Act set the ground for America's entire land grant educational system. And in a succession of following Acts, the Federal government encouraged a series of state initiatives to boost further development of agriculture, food, and lake/marine resources industries. Today, there are 215 public Land Grant educational institutions operating in the US.

Thus, in the latter part of the 19th century and through the 20th, there was significant differentiation among American universities, based on mission. Each institution would specialize in a general area: agriculture, engineering, liberal arts, etc. But during the latter period of that era, there was convergence and integration of these fields, which led to the present American system of comprehensive research universities. However, their missions began to lose their sharp focus over time. Teaching colleges grew into large, comprehensive state universities; engineering schools became technological universities. Vannevar Bush, the brilliant engineer and scientific advisor to the Roosevelt wartime administration, had a strong hand in visioning the shape and role of the modern research university.

Land grant institutions are facing tough times ahead. They must lobby their legislatures ever harder for needed funding just to stay afloat. Deficits from their state appropriations have to be made up somehow, and that means more reliance on Federal funding. This has detracted managers from their original mission of serving agricultural and industrial development. It is particularly hurting the small and medium-sized institutions, as they face new and tougher competition for research support. In their struggle to find additional research funding, what used to be teams within and across these institutions are now evolving into smaller, more isolated projects that are off-mission.

Colleges and universities, particularly in the public sector, face, and will continue to face, serious problems with funding. Foremost of these problems are financial inasmuch as they affect public higher education particularly. As will be seen in Chapter V, presidents of these institutions continue to struggle to find ways to minimize cuts from state and Federal agencies, while trying to cater to still larger cohorts of men and women of all ages. Many states face annual deficits for their academic institutions, measured in billions of dollars. This provides ample incentive for schools to be more efficient in the way they dispense educational services.

3. THE DISTINCTIVE AND CHANGING CULTURE OF THE MODERN UNIVERSITY

America now has more than 16 million students enrolled, full and part-time, at study. These students attend some 3,900 institutions consisting of two-year community colleges, and four-year, comprehensive, graduate, university and upper-level schools. The standard of these institutions' programs is carefully monitored for quality and stability, both internally and with the oversight of outside accreditation organizations. This process is vested in our well-oiled independent accreditation system. It consists of six regional bodies that are recognized by the US Education Department, by the Council for Higher Education Accreditation, and by some 80 specialized accreditation bodies which oversee the quality of these institutions—ranging from acupuncture and oriental medicine, to veterinary medicine. Each has the job of periodically monitoring the quality of the institutions for which they are responsible.

Each accreditation body consists of unbiased volunteer experts who come together periodically to inspect in detail the issues of a program's scope, leadership, faculty, relevance, student satisfaction and learning. Following each review the accreditation members provide comment and recommendations as to the program's leadership, and issue a performance rating. This process generally works well, as the accreditation members are dedicated subject experts, independent of the particular program or institution, and can help by giving of their advice and experience. More will be said about accreditation processes in Chapter III.2.

An examination of the "traditional" cohort of US college students shows that, unlike in past generations, only a minority of college students now go on and get their baccalaureate degree in four years. Each year some nine million students earn baccalaureate bachelor degrees. About 40 percent of those graduating from high school enter college directly. Many of them work part- or full-time, but their parents still shoulder much of the educational costs. Modern students play hard, yet they work harder than did those in earlier times. Some three-quarters of students work at jobs while earning a four-year degree; a quarter of those work full-time. Nearly two-thirds will earn their baccalaureate degrees within five years, 20 percent will drop out, and the rest will graduate in more than five years. And students are more mobile than ever. Of those that do graduate within five years, fewer than half (47 percent) will stay enrolled in their original institution; they will finish elsewhere. There are a variety of reasons for this, including being with close friends, finding another institution more to their liking, changing major or field of interest, or simply for convenience. These factors have implications for all institutions that wish to retain their graduates. Among them are waning loyalty, and future gifting from students who stayed at their original school.

America is rich with choices and modes of pursuing higher education. There are college and university campuses serving students at literally every corner of the map. About 1,300 of these are two-year community colleges; the rest provide baccalaureate or higher.

Such is the richness of educational and intellectual diversity, that it now threatens the future of some institutions. Most would agree that all those aspiring to some level of post-secondary education ought to be able to seek and secure it. There is now a general consensus that every American youth should pursue at least two years of college-level education in order to compete in an increasingly complex working environment.

American women are in the majority on college campuses—7.5 million of the 13.2 million undergraduates are women. And American women, for the first time, have overtaken men in completing earned doctorates. But the ascent may be specious; the statistics on women show that their degree count has stayed about the same (approximately 13,000 annually), while men's doctorates have been falling. In particular, doctorates in the physical sciences and engineering have dropped, a fact that has many people quite concerned. Some 19 percent of all doctorates earned by US citizens have been awarded to minorities. Of all the doctorates earned in the US by foreigners, the largest shares are from China, followed by South Korea, then India.

Hispanics now account for some 13 percent of US Americans. They are the largest and fastest-growing minority group in the US today, and will continue to outgrow other minority groups. They are being courted aggressively for teaching posts at colleges and universities. Some 190 colleges have been identified as "Hispanic-serving institutions"—meaning that 25 percent or more of their institution's enrollment is from this ethnic group. Another 50 schools are in Puerto Rico. As a group, Hispanics are determined to get their fair share of the American Dream. But the process is often difficult for those many families that are the first to enter college. Among the challenges are poor academic preparation, family pressures, finding financial aid, fewer students that go on to enroll in four-year institutions after finishing at two-year community colleges, and language and cultural challenges. Attrition is another factor; 44 percent of Hispanic immigrants fail to graduate high school—compared with 15 percent that are born in the US. Colleges are working hard to recruit Hispanic professors through networking and early identification of budding scholars in the nation's graduate schools.

As always, the devil lurks in the details. Post-secondary education is thought of as comprising 18- to 22-year-old students going straight from high school. These students matriculate for many different reasons: educational and career goals, family expectations, social aspects, athletics, etc. Not long ago, this cohort of mostly full-time students made up the overwhelming share of all college students. Today, that proportion has plummeted to about 16 percent. The remainder is a mix of adult learners pursuing studies through traditional and corporate universities, online adult studies via traditional and for-profit colleges and universities, and various other channels. Choices abound.

However, these choices also carry disadvantages. The traditional "right-of-passage" students are faced with such a broad palette of options that it can be quite difficult for them to choose rationally the best available. And because of the large menu given to them, they often make unwise choices. Students today most often choose a school based upon merely where their friends go, tips, geography, tuition, or simply by where they believe they can be accepted. Often, they are required to declare a major field in the first year or two, whether they are ready to or not. Students who are finishing their formal course of study are now generally faced with years of debt service. Furthermore, because of the ever-shrinking "half-life" of useful knowledge (3-10 years), young and mature students alike soon realize that continuing to learn throughout life is important to succeed in life. Yesterday's knowledge is refuse, to be discarded today and replaced tomorrow with better tools and new challenges. The flourishing business of lifelong learning, which offers continuing education during and after work hours, occupies a growing number.

As wise consumers of higher education, young scholars know the score: more education means more income. Currently in the US, a high school diploma means, on average, a lifetime income of $1.2 million. Relative to this benchmark, an undergraduate degree is worth $2.1 million; a master's degree $2.5 million, a doctorate $3.4 million, and a professional degree (law, medicine, etc.) $4.4 million. Today's college graduates earn nearly twice the salaries of those having no more than a high-school diploma.

Changes are coming in higher education, which will be examined in detail in the ensuring chapters of this book. But before proceeding, the following is an analogy by Dr. R. Byron Pipes, former President of the Rensselaer Polytechnic Institute, New York. He tells the story of the transition from vaudeville theater to motion picture entertainment. In earlier times, companies of actors at each of hundreds of local stages across America practiced the art of vaudeville. These local companies flourished as the main channel of amusement throughout the 19th and into the mid-20th centuries. But with the advent of motion pictures, the game suddenly changed. Local motion picture theaters had no need for producers or actors. Although a few vaudeville actors were able to make the transition to traveling companies, most were unable to move into the new media. They simply were replaced by technology, and had to find other work. Nothing abides, and the present educational era is morphing into still another.

This tale begs the analogy with the esteemed professor, teaching in his/her classroom or lab. What will be the proper role of information technology in the years ahead? Will it be in the form of streaming video, web-enabled pedagogy, or virtual experiments, etc.? To what extent will it—or should it—erode the need for this venerable professor, today's "sage on the stage"? Might virtual lectures and discussions with world-class professors, such as the late and famed Caltech physics professor Richard Feynman, replace the need for physical faculty at each and every college in the US? Is it possible that, before long, great teachers will be franchised, while others slowly disappear? Heresy? Consider the analogy of hand-crafted book making in the aftermath of the Gutenberg printing press. Surely the cheap availability of books and online content has long made the old methods obsolete. Americans honor change and progress, and intellectual and market-based achievement. These and other provocative and emotional issues will be discussed throughout the rest of this book.[3]

Another change is being witnessed within the cultures of colleges and universities, and of the communities in which they operate. Academic institutions have long had reputations of being insular—communities that operate within, but largely apart from their own neighborhoods. These "gown-town" schisms have led to significant and ongoing quarrels in many campus communities, large and small. They are two cultures thrown together with not much in common and often with high walls between them. For one thing, most of these institutional properties are not on the tax roll, which pushes local taxes ever higher. This is particularly onerous in smaller communities where a large academic presence dominates. Pressure for affordable student housing drives residents out of the local community, to outlying areas. These community disruptions have become legendary in cities from Cambridge, to Ann Arbor, to Palo Alto.

But there are signs of change. It may have started with Duke University where, in the mid-nineties, officials decided that the university owed a "special obligation" to faculty seeking affordable housing. This trend is now well under way in other venues and provisions for increases in adjunct faculty are being made by offering such faculty fixed-term (typically, five years) renewable contracts. It may be controversial but it

---

3. "The Role of Information Technology in 21st Century Education," from an Address by R. Byron Pipes, 2000.

is effective. Duke has since invested more than $2 million in loan funds for housing for the poor, and has opened a clinic for elementary-school children. Other colleges—from the University of Pennsylvania, to Marquette University and the University of Southern California—are taking similar steps. Many other private and public universities are following suit, acknowledging the need and value of bringing these two disparate communities together for mutual benefit.[4]

Another significant change in higher education is taking place through shifts within academic governance. Starting in the economic boom time of the 1980s, many colleges began to change their attitudes, towards more businesslike principles in authority levels and performance measurement. Roger W. Bowen, President of the State University of New York at New Paltz, describes this trend as having "turned university presidents into chief executive officers, provosts into chief operating officers, and vice presidents for administration into chief financial officers. Deans have become middle management and departments, lower-level management. Faculty members are now labor, and students are consumers, or clients." He argues that boards of trustees, mainly business leaders, have seen the need to enact comprehensive reform. Indeed, there is now a subtle shift toward principles of accountability and efficiency—a shift abhorrent to many traditional academics who generally see the enemy as those who would "remake academe in the image of the corporation." Dr. Bowen goes on to say that underlying these trends is "a suspicion of academe and its arcane traditions; its inefficient, labor-intensive ways of educating students; its practice of lifetime employment through tenure; its procedures of shared governance. Those who favor the corporate model see higher education as a social atavism sorely in need of comprehensive reform."

The concept of shared governance is a core value of all American colleges and universities. It protects faculty and administrators from top-down authority and brings security to the institution. It is participatory and collegial. But the mounting financial and competitive pressures on institutions have caused a few cracks in the dike. For example, in the late

---

4. "Charity Moves Off-Campus," in *The Economist*, Dec. 4, 1999, pg. 31.

1990s Barat College, a 4-year, private Catholic liberal arts college in Lake Forest, Illinois, openly opted for a directed governance model. Some 30 administers were dismissed in order to tighten their belt, and in the process, their culture and values were radically changed. This is elaborated on in Chapter V.

Undoubtedly the introduction of educational technology is shifting the faculty's role from teacher to coach. Faculty members, armed with new and more potent technologies, are taking different teaching approaches. They are finding that often the best instructional approach is to return to the Socratic Method. In this, learning is based on the teacher posing provocative questions which arouse curiosity and stimulate students to find the answer themselves, in logical, incremental steps. This "inquiry-based" method of teaching, in which students find the answers under general guidance of the "coach," is becoming the preferred choice of many educators. It is much more powerful than having students passively taking notes from an instructor delivering a lecture. A pioneer in this method of instruction is the Illinois Mathematics & Science Academy, a world-class, residential high school for gifted students, in Aurora.

Murray Sperber, Indiana University Professor of Labor & Management, advocates the abolishment of teaching methods which turn students into passive receptacles. Instead, he and others call for colleges and universities to promote interactive, inquiry-based learning. He, and a growing chorus of academics, simply wants to end the lecture-course system and replace it with smaller classes wherein students and faculty member constantly interact.

Moreover this approach to learning, when coupled with new educational technology, can be delivered less expensively. It is the newest link in a chain of successive educational improvements over the centuries. Although the tutorial system of Oxford and Cambridge was highly effective in its time, it is now enormously expensive when applied to today's egalitarian cultures.

On the other hand, students must ultimately learn for themselves. The very technologies which afford a richer educational environment by working in teams, help reinforce the value of individual learning.

Whereas the Socratic approach put the master in front of his students, now students are increasingly untethering themselves from the professor via asynchronous learning. They can learn and apply what they read in books and in content via the web, and do so at any time and in any place. As Frank Mayadas, Program Director of the Sloan Foundation, states, Abraham Lincoln is believed to have attended classes a total of just 12 months in his entire life, achieving his credentials in law, and an unsurpassed mastery of the English language, mainly by reading books and manuscripts on his own. And Mayadas further cites the Indian postal clerk Srinivasa Ramanujan who, in the early 1900s, learned practically the entire field of mathematics, and developed original theorems, with knowledge gained only from books.[5]

Now, of course, there are many new educational tools and paradigms, made possible by technological advances, facilitating better pedagogy, and allowing students to learn and understand much better. But it has also begun to change fundamentally the role of the teacher/instructor. As will be seen in later chapters, it has enabled the teachers who are comfortable with using these (often capricious) technologies to do a much better job of educating students. Colleges and universities are searching for effective ways to retrain faculty so that they can make proper use of both the technology and the new learning styles to improve knowledge accretion. It is a big challenge, but one that will be met.

Improvement comes with a cost. As mentioned earlier, the eras of post-World War II and the Korean conflict discharged a flood of eager, mature men and women students onto campuses, mostly as undergraduates. To cope with this influx—and to deliver quality education—larger lecture classrooms, augmented by smaller recitation rooms and laboratories, were required. For the first time educators were driven to economies of scale. Larger institutions were heaviest affected, having to cope with new capital programs for dorms, classrooms and other facilities. For these universities, quality began to suffer. Graduate programs faired com-

---

5. "Asynchronous Learning Network Programs," an address by Frank Mayadas at the University of Illinois at Urbana, Sept. 20, 2001.

paratively better, as student growth rates were small, and growing Federal research programs carried more of the load.

But the bubble burst when the last "baby boomers" left the campuses, and universities still had to cover their fixed costs including, of course, tenured faculty and existing infrastructure. The income shortfalls could not all be accommodated by tuition increases. For the first time in memory, administrators were forced to reckon with program efficiencies and cutbacks. Leaderships clamored for ways to keep the academic ship afloat financially, without degrading educational quality and reputation.

These forces of change will always exist. In the long term, it is vital that institutions think creatively of how to respond to various economic cycles and to rising tuitions and other costs. From a business perspective, it is essential that institutions develop more options in order to balance their business. This is increasingly happening.

A closer look at what students are opting to study, in relation to national needs, reveals some worrying trends. One significant cause of concern is that fewer students are pursing programs in science and technology. Simply put, these programs are more difficult and costly to administer than most others, and the marketplace has not yet provided appropriate information and incentives to encourage students to commit to such programs. If this trend continues, there could be a long-term impact on US competitiveness. Since the beginning of the industrial age land, labor and capital have been the engines driving economic progress. But in the modern era a fourth ingredient—technology—needs to be added to the mix of skills required year after year.

According to the National Science Foundation, US colleges awarded more bachelors degrees in the period 1987-97 than in any other decade, although the numbers awarded technical degrees plummeted significantly. During that period 37 percent fewer degrees in computer science were awarded, 24 percent fewer in math and 16 percent fewer in engineering. And although US graduate degrees overall increased that decade, it was largely because of the influx of foreign students to the US to fill the seats in science and engineering classrooms. Furthermore, technical programs are more expensive to run because of equipment costs, faculty salaries and the greater requirement for one-on-one teacher-student relationships to help students with highly complex ideas. The problems of waning interest and the increasing cost of engineering and science programs are causing many institutions to curtail and even withdraw these programs. And recent efforts on behalf of the Federal military branches to address this problem with more stipends and other support have not made any material difference.

It is not only science and engineering that are suffering. Colleges and universities are turning out insufficient numbers of graduates that will be needed for the New Economy. More and more pressure is being put on institutions to provide lifelong education, or to adopt "cradle-to-post-retirement" approaches. It can be seen that the education industry is growing at an annual rate of about 5-6 percent but certain sectors will soon grow at nearly triple that pace. They range from businesses providing kindergartens, to those supplying computers to high schools. And the emerging educational markets that deliver specialized college or professional degrees are booming, as growing numbers of high school graduates and working adults seek education at nontraditional for-profit schools such as DeVry and the University of Phoenix.

The number of projected full- and part-time college students is fast expanding from a trough of 2.2 million students in 1992, to about 3.2 million by 2004. And 44 percent of those students are now working adults over the age of 24. They are highly mobile: some 60 percent of college students will have attended more that one institution before their graduation. The ability to deliver college and professional certification courses over the Internet is generating an almost breathless rush to feed this appetite via private, for-profit and traditional schools as with Sylvan and MCI WorldCom, Inc.'s joint ventures. Also, Caliber Learning Network, Inc., which took their program public in May, 1998 with the goal of providing distance learning for professionals in classrooms, is thriving. They have signed deals with Johns Hopkins University and the Wharton School at the University of Pennsylvania to deliver medical and business courses around the country.

But the industry is learning that it cannot take corporate customers for granted. A common problem is that industrial companies often do not become repeat buyers of courses without regular follow-up and, often, in-class teaching and customization. Too many companies are designing products without regard to the customers' needs and how they will be used, warns Matthew Feldman, managing director of Learning Insights, which offers CD-ROM finance products. This fast-emerging market has little tolerance for such shortsightedness.[6]

4. Creating Knowledge Workers

Americans are a very practical people. As the new "information age" gets underway, curricula will become ever more practical. And as the half-life of knowledge gets ever shorter, colleges and universities will be increasingly expected to provide continuing education. There will be increased competition among for-profit and corporate university enterprises. Employers increasingly will provide not degrees *per se*, but rather knowledge, capabilities and advanced skills that can be used in a practical way. They are developing reliable ways to test for knowledge standards and for useful skills among all employees.

Philip Condit, former CEO of the Boeing Company, sees three basic principles evolving. Firstly, academe and industry will continue to converge, spurred on largely by market globalization. Secondly, education will be continuous as new practices are adopted and those that are no longer useful are discarded. And thirdly, educational standards will evolve beyond current accreditation standards, and closer to a quality assurance model aimed at betterment and *kaizen*—the Japanese notion of continuous improvement. New and more potent educational technologies will continue to be developed, and will thread their ways through all fields of knowledge.[7]

---

6. *Business Week*, Jan. 11, 1999, pp. 132-133.
7. "The Global University," by Philip Condit and R. Byron Pipes, *Issues in Science and Technology*, Vol. XIV, Number 1, 1997, pp. 27-28.

This vision resonates well with the concept of mass educational customization, a notion borrowed from the marketing of consumer products. It leads with thoughts of providing tailored education, and an acknowledgment that different people learn in different ways and at different speeds. The current "e-Generation" of students, for example, is much more visually oriented than those of past generations because of the hyper-video culture. Technologies and practices are being developed that will enable people of every age to learn continuously, more efficiently and enjoyably. This is but another phase in the quest to stay in step with the increasingly hi-tech/hi-touch environment, as foretold in the 1982 blockbuster *Megatrends*, by John Naisbitt and Patricia Aburdene. There is an enormous market potential for educational tools, and that will certainly challenge traditional learning standards.

There is now more experimentation with undergraduate curricula, aimed at equipping students with a wider understanding of various fields of study, whether in the classics or engineering. More attention is being paid to differentiating programs that will appeal to particular student market segments, and to offering something different. In perhaps the boldest ever curricula review among undergraduate liberal arts/science programs, Harvard University recently recommended sweeping changes in their undergraduate curriculum. The highlights of their seven proposals are:

- Encourage every student to complete an "international experience" that would include study, research or work abroad.
- Replace the current core program of general education classes with a new, as yet undefined, series of courses that would be interdisciplinary and that might include requirements in the humanities, social sciences, life sciences and physical sciences.
- Decrease the number of requirements for a "major" concentration of study and delay the choice of the major until the middle of the sophomore year. (The decision is currently made in the freshman year.)
- Create an office to coordinate academic advising.
- Establish a January term in which students are free from examinations and can study, do field or volunteer work, or pursue innovative courses.
- Emphasize smaller classes for undergraduates, starting with a required small-group seminar in the first year that is to be led by senior faculty members.

Jack Forstadt, a Human Resources consultant, makes the important point that the need for knowledge workers will increasingly outstrip the need for traditional physical workers. This new breed of workers must be able to continue improving their performance far longer than their physical-labor counterparts. They generally will work considerably beyond customary retirement ages—into their 70s and 80s—and will have more leisure years ahead. Furthermore, the means of production will increasingly be intellectual, not physical. It will be the workers, not the companies in which they work, that will ultimately own their production methods. And as a result of these factors, and shrinking employee loyalties, people will work for more companies and will develop larger toolkits of skills.

In fact, some of these forecasts are coming together today. The business of continuing education for adults is growing at astonishing rates. As mentioned previously, five of every six persons now pursuing college courses are over 25 years of age. And most of them are taking their studies through unconventional channels, such as online and corporate universities. Is it any surprise, then, that there is unprecedented competition among traditional colleges and universities, more mergers and closures (now about two every year across America), and much more attention to cost efficiencies and institutional "branding" as a needed marketing tool?

All of this means troubled waters ahead for traditional colleges and universities that are not prepared to work within an environment of continual change. As costs continue to rise well above inflation rates, the only survival option is that dreaded word *efficiency*. For many reasons, as will be explored further in later chapters, the statistics are sobering. As noted earlier, costs are rising well above inflation rates and consumer price indices. They simply cannot continue unabated. Those institutions that find appropriate means of curtailing escalating costs will be the winners; the rest, followers. Staff support roles will also be put under pressure to become more lean and efficient.

These factors all conspire to place enormous pressures on respected educational systems—undisputedly the best in the world. Tough questions are being asked: status of tenure, closer collaborations and outsourcing arrangements with the corporate sector, and the resulting dilution of control. The challenge is to educate more efficiently and with greater focus; and to respond to the rising student chorus for more choice in pursuing the individual's education plans. These and other issues will be explored in more detail in later chapters.

Chapter III: Beginnings of the New Transformation

Process, Process, Process

>Topical Themes
>1. The Input Side: K-12 Education
>2. Accreditation of Colleges and Universities
>3. The Structure of Colleges and Universities
>4. Admissions: Gatekeepers, Diversity & Affirmative Action
>5. The Learning Environment
>6. Pedagogy: Trends and Measuring Educational Outcomes

1. The Input Side: K-12 Education

    The message being conveyed in this book is that higher education in the future will be very much different than in the past. Indeed, more change has taken place in the past two decades than in the past two millennia. It is tempting simply to extrapolate from past experience in order to forecast the future. As Yogi Berra used to say, "prediction is hard, especially about the future." The art of extrapolation in order to see the future has been around since the ancient Greeks. But even they knew the folly of foretelling the future from past experience. Mark Twain once satirized the art of prediction by saying that Cairo, Illinois and New Orleans will become contiguous sister cities some 650 years from now, because the lower Mississippi River is slowly straightening its meandering kinks.

But the changes referred to here cannot be anticipated by simple extrapolation. It is about *revolutionary* change. There is even a new term for such kinds of momentous shifts, coined by Harvard Business School's Clayton Christensen: *disruption*. Christensen and his disciples have discussed disruption in the context of new technologies that overnight change the present order of products and services. Familiar business and social practices are rendered obsolete very quickly. That is what is happening now; a new era is dawning in which there will be profound differences in the way higher education is delivered. And it will be much better for it.

Before the future of higher education can be foreseen, there must first be an understanding of current bedrock educational processes. There is no question that the provision of excellent primary and secondary education to all citizens is vital. The entire system of higher education depends on it. But an examination of the details and complexity of K-12 processes reveals more cracks—and new opportunities.

Here is a snapshot of the K-12 educational system. The education pipeline begins with the 108,000 public and private elementary and secondary schools. The public system enrolls about 35 million K-8 children in some 70,000 schools; high school pupils in grades 9-12 make up another 15 million students, attending about 20,000 schools. The number of high school graduates has risen steadily since 1992, and will peak in 2009. Private secular and religious schools provide for the education of another 6 million or so elementary and high school students. Demographic forecasts indicate that, overall, the number of primary students will remain steady, but that secondary enrollments will grow by about 4 percent a year in the short term. This raises a particular concern, namely: will the capacity to deliver quality primary and secondary school content continue to be squeezed because enrollments will outstrip funding for school construction, teachers and budgets? Additionally, the growing popularity of alternative schools reduces somewhat the growth needs of the secondary school system, a point that will be looked at later.

Americans continue to search for better ways to provide educational programs that will match the diversity and intellectual quality that children will need to succeed in life. There are some interesting benchmarks. Achievement data from the US and other nations have consistently shown that American students fall well short of what they need in order to have better options in life. This gap is especially troublesome in the fields of mathematics and science. Students in top-ranked Singapore, the world's leader both in mathematics and science, score well above US students: the *average* science/math student in Singapore scores about the same as the *top 10 percent* of US scholars. The math content of US 8th-grade classes is at a 7th-grade level compared with most other countries. Craig Barrett, former CEO of Intel Corp., says that when high school graduates among the world's top 25 countries are compared, the American grade school student scores, on average, near the bottom 10% overall in mathematics. The good news is, however, that American students are on the top rung in terms of creative thinking.[8]

Senator John Glenn, Chair of the National Commission on Mathematics and Science Teaching for the 21st Century, in a speech at Harvard University expressed his concern that there are too few math and science teachers at the K-12 level, and that those who do teach the subjects are often unqualified for the job. Nationally, more than one-quarter of math teachers and 56 percent of science teachers are teaching outside their fields of expertise. Despite their small size, liberal arts colleges are equipped, on a per capita basis, to produce nearly twice as many students who go on to earn a PhD in science as other institutions. Liberal arts graduates also are disproportionately represented in the leadership of the scientific community. In a recent two-year period, nearly 20 percent of scientists elected to the prestigious National Academy of Sciences received their undergraduate education at liberal arts colleges. What accounts for this success? It seems to be due, in large part, to their emphasis on hands-on, laboratory-rich science from the introductory level onward. If there is to be hope for the future of science education in America, it lies in the recognition of the value of inquiry-based learning

---

8. "Liberal arts key to science equation," in *The Chicago Sun-Times*, April 21, 2001, p. 18.

which prepares students not only to be scientifically literate, but also to be better teachers and better informed leaders and citizens.

American youth are increasingly falling behind, as measured by many international standards of academic achievement. It is easy to blame crowded schools, under-prepared teachers, an overemphasis on athletics and inadequate budgets for contributing to nine percent of young people dropping out of high school. These are certainly serious concerns. But although these are factors in the quality-of-education equation, the fundamental cause is quite clear: Studies by the Council on Competitiveness, and others, show that there is a clear relationship between the number of days a year spent in math classes, and the students' achievements in that skill. Students simply do not have as many "seat hours" per year as children in other developed countries. In the US, the average academic year for high school students is about 178 days. In comparison, Italy, Israel, Germany, Japan, Taiwan and Korea each require more than 200 days attendance; China requires 250 days. US society still clings to its old farmland traditions of using children to help with the sowing and reaping. It still reaps what it sows, but more so now in the context of stronger intellectual prowess than crops. Each fall, teachers spend, on average, two to three weeks covering material that has already been learned but then forgotten during the course of long childhood summers. The issue of how many school days are required in a school year needs to be addressed seriously.

For Americans, the commitment to longer school years has had good, but difficult, consequences. Parents, by and large, do not support such measures for they interfere with work and vacation schedules. Moreover, stretching out the school year directly impacts on state budgets; it is estimated that going from a 180- to a 220-day academic calendar requires an increase of 40 percent in budget spending. Nevertheless, many US school districts are experimenting with the concept of longer school years, a practice that will likely become more widespread.

These are just some of the more prominent causes of the educational challenges throughout K-12. Serious reform is called for. Among those advocating improvement is Lockheed Martin CEO Norman Augustine, who headed the Education Task Force of the *Business Roundtable*. He laments, "There is ample evidence that our curricula and expectations for our young people are not demanding enough." The challenge facing America's schools is the empowerment of all children to function effectively in their future, a future marked increasingly by change, information growth, and evolving technologies.[9] Unlike in any other era, today's students must plan for lifetime learning in order to have a successful career. And technology will have a huge influence on changing and improving student learning.

Also demanding attention is the requirement for more and better-qualified teachers to meet the needs of the student population. America's 1,300 teacher training institutions must prepare, in the next decade, to produce over 2.2 million new teachers to fill the nation's classrooms, at a rate of approximately 220,000 per year. Facing a projected shortfall of teachers in the years ahead, community colleges in at least 20 States are gearing up to train prospective elementary and secondary school educators. In fact one community college, Florida's St. Petersburg College, has State approval to offer bachelor's degrees in teacher education. Other two-year colleges are expected to win similar approval. The fact is that some 40 percent of teachers have completed some portion of their undergraduate work at community colleges. This makes such a bold step quite appropriate.

A recent study of American higher education, and its underpinnings from K-12 schools, has revealed three major characteristics and behaviors which appear to have most greatly influenced students' access to and success in four-year colleges and universities[10]:

Academic Preparation and Performance: A rigorous high school program yields long-lasting benefits. Taking challenging academic courses not only helps students get into college, but also increases their likelihood of succeeding. Although high school students may find it difficult to look so

---

9. National Educational Technology: Standards for Students, International Society for Technology in Education, 2000.
10. "Access & Persistence: Findings from 10 Years of Longitudinal Research on Students," by Susan P. Choy, American Council on Education, Center for Policy Analysis, Washington, D.C., 2002.

far ahead, they need to know that what they do in high school truly counts. Opting for an easier schedule might boost one's grade point average (GPA), but as a strategy it is unlikely to pay off in the long term.

Parent's Education: Students whose parents did not go to college are themselves less likely to enroll in college or persist toward a bachelor's degree than their peers with college-educated parents. This is true even when accounting for other factors such as income, educational expectations, academic preparation, parental involvement, and peer influence. However, for first-generation college students who do overcome these barriers, earning a bachelor's degree seems to level the playing field in their first few years after graduation. Parental education had little or no impact.

Nontraditional Status: Many college students come to campus already bearing adult burdens, such as full-time jobs and/or dependents to support. For example, if a student is a parent, he or she is more likely to work full time and attend school part time—and more often will not complete a bachelor's degree. Also, these students follow their own way with regard to work and study. They face difficult challenges but usually emerge stronger and more confident, whether or not they complete their degree.

Still another issue that demands attention is that of teacher salaries and how to retain and bring out the best in teachers, against the lure of other professions which pay better. Kati Haycock, Founder and Director of the Education Trust, calls for incentives such as scholarships and loan forgiveness for professionals committed to teaching in high poverty schools. She also calls for rewards for top teacher graduates, and for those who use non-traditional but rigorous routes into the profession, such as retired military and executives.

At the center of the issue of better education is the sad but fundamental fact that in America, the status of teachers only receives lip service. Yet these dedicated people are, by and large, true heroes. Ironically, they are generally underpaid and overworked, and lack the social status and respect they richly deserve.

The following is an illustration of how the teaching profession is really viewed. Some years back, the author's daughter was a student at New Trier High School, in Winnetka, Chicago, one of the top public schools in America. She asked him to accompany her to their annual, semiformal evening event to which all fathers were invited to have dinner and a social with their daughters in the school's auditorium. As the family had only recently moved into the neighborhood, he did not know any of the other fathers attending. His daughter and he took their seats at one of the dinner tables and made efforts to join in with this tight-knit group as they swapped stories of their exploits as physicians, corporate bigwigs and attorneys. Finally, as a courtesy, one father across the table from him asked what he did for a living. He said simply that he was a school teacher, an answer that evoked a clear, nonverbal response which dripped with an "oh, I'm sorry" attitude. His new table companion then felt obligated to follow up by asking him where he taught. It was only when he said that he was a professor and department chair at a major Chicago university that the others lit up. He was then deemed to be "OK." They continued chatting, but that subtle exchange spoke volumes to the author. As a "high school teacher" he would have been a mere interloper in this group of fast-track dads, but as a professor he had a bit of respect.

So, what is the recipe for school improvement? The most important ingredient is the placement of the best teachers in front of those students who most need quality instruction. Reasonable salaries and bonuses, incentives and recognition will aid retention. It is an unfortunate fact that there are far too many under qualified teachers trying to educate future citizens and leaders. Authorities in the field have cited four key indicators of teaching excellence: high scores in students' achievement tests; a deep knowledge of the subject they teach; effective teaching skills; and a continuous improvement in those skills through individual effort and in collaboration with their peers. To this may be added a genuine interest or passion for education. One creative and successful approach is New York City's program for designating peer coaches to help raise the quality of instruction in their schools. The desire is not to evaluate or grade teacher performance, but rather to help and coach teachers to reach their highest potential. This approach is starting to take root in some colleges and universities.

How is good teaching to be defined? Sam Pickering, professor of English at the University of Connecticut, put it succinctly: by lesson preparation, discipline and mood; by trust and the engagement of all students, not just the confident; by shared understandings among students and teachers, truth, and making the subject alive and relevant; and by the avoidance of exaggerations and distortions.

Another difficult issue—arguably a national tragedy—is the gap between children of different socio-economic and racial backgrounds. The fact is that children of all races, national origins and socio-economic stations, are smart, can excel in school and can perform academically just as well as others, given equal learning environments—provided that the school system does not fail them. The exceptions to this fact are the children who are slow to learn because of special intellectual, emotional or social handicaps. Of course there are differences. On the reading and math sections of the National Assessment of Educational Progress (NAEP), 17-year-old African-American and Hispanic students typically score at the same level as 13-year-old Caucasian children. However, credible data from studies of children has shown definitively that these two groups show no difference in comparison with the performance of white middle-class students of the same age *when given the same quality and level of learning programs*. Essentially, it is not the children who fail but the system, and some teachers, that fail them.

The two key means for narrowing the achievement gap are teacher quality and accountability. Proper teacher training, recruitment, assignment, and professional development can improve the standards of underperforming children. Teachers know that the difference between a good and a bad teacher can be shown in the level of achievement in a single school year and that a poor teacher will handicap a child for years. Moreover, the more talented teachers often earn the right to choose a less challenging assignment, not a more demanding one. What is needed is a durable process wherein the best teachers are properly encouraged and induced to apply their skills to those students, including those in inner city schools, who most need them. Kati Haycock has said that ingenuity must be used to achieve this.[11]

Yet a further problem lies in the way schools are designed. Studies as far back as the 1950s have shown that larger schools make students feel isolated and lost; less powerful and less confident. They do not feel a connection with the school environment, and that directly affects their ability to learn. It contributes to indifference and poor academic performance.

Awareness is also increasing of another, quite disturbing dimension: bullying. There has always been bullying, but now it is getting meaner. The good news is that it is finally drawing the media attention it deserves.

This rather gloomy state of affairs for the K-12 population has led to a rapid increase in the number of parents who are taking personal charge of their children's education by teaching them at home, and to the rise of private schooling. Since the early 1970s there has been a surge of independent day schools, offering an alternative to public high schools. It is now perfectly legal in the United States to educate children at home. This trend continues, with enrollments growing yearly at about 20 percent. More than 2 million children are now being taught by their parents at home instead of in traditional public or private schools. Some four percent of all K-12 children are home-schooled, and now outnumber costly boarding school enrollments by about 4:1.

Related to this trend is the growth of virtual schooling. Here, the medium is the Internet and materials from providers are aimed specifically at either side of the norm for school children: those with special needs as well as the gifted. Each week, virtual schools provide materials, online or via mail, with structured lessons and tests. These programs can provide tailored pacing for students but may lack the social environment that is important to these children.

Children taught at home are largely from middle-class, faith-based families, although non-believers also are included in this movement. This mode of education is proving to be quite effective; children who are

---

11. Texas Lone State, Vol. 19, No. 6, Aug/Sept/2001.

schooled at home tend, as a group, to be more successful in their college years and beyond. Moreover, many home-school companies, such as eSylvan, offer content materials and guidance to families opting for this form of education. Such products are also available on the Internet and in bookstores.

This topic ends with another personal story from the author, again from New Trier High School. It illustrates how the bureaucratic school system sometimes gets in the way of delivering good education to children. One day, word went out from Chicago radio stations about a teachers' strike, and a plea was made for substitute teachers to come in and cover until the strike ended. As the father of four children then attending the school, the author responded to the challenge by calling the school's superintendent and offering to cover their calculus classes until the crisis ended, free of charge. The superintendent was grateful, and then asked him if he was a state-certified teacher. He told her no, but that he was a professor with a doctorate in applied mathematics and had got top marks from students for his teaching skills. There was a pause, and then she said that she appreciated the gesture but could not accept the author's offer because he was not officially qualified to teach, even during a period of crisis. Fortunately, the strike ended quickly.

2. Accreditation of Colleges and Universities

One aspect of great learning institutions is the system of accreditation, by which schools maintain and continuously improve intellectual integrity.

Accreditation is an independent process that oversees the quality, stability and relevance of colleges and universities. It is vital in helping institutions to avoid a lowering of standards, which would result in them becoming weaker and less competitive. The purpose of accreditation is to assure continuing quality of programs by periodic visits of expert panelists who examine closely program content, curricula, quality and integrity. Typically, each US college and university is visited every two to four years and provides a report on its purpose, programs and services.

An audit is then conducted of the institution and its major components. Each major component of the institution (Arts and Sciences, Engineering, Medicine, etc.) is responsible for keeping its own accreditation intact by continuously improving its internal processes. At the end of this review process, the visiting committee provides its findings and recommendations, aimed at strengthening that component.

Most accreditation processes are done on a regional basis, except for the State of New York, which has the only state agency accreditation body. Other than New York, accreditation is managed by one of the six regional associations of schools and colleges: Middle States, New England, North Central, Northwest, Southern, and Western. These authorities are recognized either by the US Department of Education or by the Council for Higher Education Accreditation. In addition, there are some 80 specialized accreditation bodies that oversee the quality of various institutions. These regional associations have real influence and authority in areas of curricula and institutional policies.

Accredition standards are foremost concerned with institutional inputs and outputs, and not so much with academic results. Accreditation certainly does not ensure academic quality, but it does play a benign policing role in elevating the standards of higher education. It is advisory and has no enforcement powers. That means that the free market has a stronger arm in shaping the institution's future than has accreditation.

The evolving process of accreditation does not, in fact, elevate academic rigor. Indeed, evidence abounds that students generally are graduating with weaker understanding of the liberal arts and sciences than some 30 years ago. According to George Leef, Director of Higher Education Policy for the American Council of Trustees and Alumni, accrediting standards, which are overwhelmingly concerned with institutional inputs and processes rather than academic results, have done nothing to arrest current trends. Most studies point to a decline in the understanding of basic academic content. Moreover, students need incentives to graduate early, or at least, on time. There is a growing population of students who, for various reasons, adopt a leisurely pace through their college years. Some have to for reasons of jobs, child rearing and other commitments. But still there is an increase in those who just want to take their time, and are in no hurry to leave the campus. This is a new phenomenon, a kind of constipation that slows the efficient throughput of students. At the University of Texas, for example, only 39 percent of undergraduate students graduate within the traditional four years. This is typical of most other institutions.

The bottom line is that accreditation is important in the sense that a college or program lacking accreditation may not excel in terms of its faculty, facilities and programs. On the other hand, many fresh new programs may be quite good yet lack a history of accomplishment. As with any investment, the buyer should examine the details of non-accredited programs to assure that it meets or exceeds expectations.

3. THE STRUCTURE OF COLLEGES AND UNIVERSITIES

Higher Education now is Big Business. As mentioned earlier, there are more than 16 million full- and part-time students enrolled in the US. They attend some 3,900 institutions, consisting of two-year community or "junior" colleges, four-year comprehensive, graduate, university and upper level professional schools. At the base of the higher education structure is the system of community colleges. These institutions account for some 41 percent of students. In the State of California some three-quarters of all public college students are enrolled in these community colleges. The forte of these institutions is in providing students with better jobs and futures. Research aimed at creating new physical or cultural knowledge is not in the remit of the community college.

Table 3.1 Distribution of America's college students:

Two-Year	41.4%
Four-Year	4.8%
Comprehensive	23.6%
Graduate	1.1%
University	28.4%
Upper level	0.7%
Total	100.0%

As Americans see continuing education as vital to their economic future, public community colleges are expanding at an unprecedented rate. No longer the preserve of those just out of high school and young adults seeking better futures, these institutions now serve people of all ages by providing the means to upgrade their skills and develop new ones. Now, states cannot build new capacity fast enough. In fact the explosion in demand for community colleges has created a new entity: the upgraded traditional community college offering four-year baccalaureate degrees. The State of Florida has seen this as a necessity, as it has strong capacity in its wide network of community colleges, but relatively few four-year institutions.

There is even a budding new market for mini master and certificate degree programs. These nontraditional programs are aimed at mid-career adults who wish to explore specific professional fields, such as informatics, gerontology, journalism. These programs are open to all students, without having to go through the usual admission stages. This is just another example of forward looking institutions offering programs which appeal to adults seeking continuous, lifetime learning experiences.

Florida now sees a strong network of senior colleges as crucial to its economic interests. And other states, including Arkansas, Nevada, Utah and Vermont, are considering them, following Miami-Dade County's model in offering bachelor's degrees. Community college leaders and lawmakers are studying this option because local industries need workers with skills that universities do not generally provide. Moreover, a growing number of students say the universities often are not accessible anyway.

On the other hand, this movement may have an uncertain future. The forte of community colleges, after all, is teaching, enabling students to gain a general intellectual preparation for pursing jobs and careers. Expanding to four-year programs would likely change fundamentally the character of the institution, to a new kind that would stress tools and techniques rather than concepts and creations. Some see this as a slippery slope, as the culture of baccalaureate institutions tends toward research, not community service. But it could succeed if these new age colleges keep their primary mission of providing improved community services.

The modern undergraduate student is far different from those in the past. In earlier times, students went from high school straight to college, studied full time, and were aided by parents for tuitions, fees and living costs. They graduated in four years and then sought gainful and permanent employment. But in the new century, only 27 percent of college students fit this profile. The rest are older, have family and work obligations, and are seeking either to enter the workplace, or take their careers to a higher level.

Another trend involves America's private two-year colleges, which are increasingly fading away. In the 1940s, public two-year colleges were about even in number with their private four-year counterparts. But now, America's current publicly supported two-year colleges number about 1,122 and are about 87 percent publicly supported. The private market share has declined from about 50 percent in the 1940s to 13 percent today. Further forcing the hand of the private two-year colleges, a two-year degree does not carry the weight in the marketplace it once did. In addition, many of the remaining community colleges are in small, often remote, towns. A few of the privates have become four-year liberal arts colleges, but the transition is costly and takes time.

But if community college systems are generally doing well, even thriving, senior institutions generally are struggling and will continue to do so. They are faced with the need to provide new patterns of learning as workers stay in the workforce longer and must continuously upgrade their skills. They are shackled by increasing costs, new competitors and content delivery services, and their inability to become more inclusive of age groups of 30 years and older. Some fear that this will harm their' future, leaving them to battle against younger competitors who can deliver lifelong practical knowledge on demand.

Chapter V will include a look at the remarkable explosion of for-profit colleges—among them Career Education Corp., Corinthian Colleges, Inc., DeVry, the University of Phoenix Online (Apollo Group), Education Management Corp., ITT Technical Institute, Sylvan Learning

Systems, Strayer University, the Corinthian Colleges and Whitman Education Group. These and other players are both enlarging the market for academic and skill-based knowledge, and taking market share from traditional colleges and universities. Their forte lies in practical education that can be applied today. They tend to be relatively low in cost, flexible (much of the content is through e-learning networks) and provide practical tools and skills. Such organizations know that their students' allegiance will keep them coming back to hone their skills and learn new ones.

The new wave students are blending their work and studies to be more efficient and personally rewarding. Some are choosing new for-profit schools that springing up across the country, serving K through graduate and professional education. These schools now constitute some 46 percent of all post-secondary institutions and some 38 percent of all institutions at which students may receive Federal financial aid. Moreover, about half of those for-profit institutions are eligible to provide Title IV Federal financial aid for their students. Congress, working through the Internal Revenue Service, is now catching up to give favorable and equal tax treatment to tuition savings plans, and level the playing field for all students pursuing legitimate college programs.

There are some educators who are uncomfortable with the revolution in the provision of higher education. Typical of this position is Jennifer Washburn's book.[12] Ms. Washburn decries what she sees as something akin to a nefarious plot to tear down traditional universities and replace them with corporate institutions bent upon the overthrow of liberal arts curricula. But the Big Brother notion has long since yielded to market forces, to a wider band of students of all ages and of various educational needs. These students vote with their feet. They save their money and time to prepare themselves in academic programs that best fulfill their personal needs, whether public, private or for-profit.

---

12. "University, Inc.: The Corporation Corruption of American Higher Education," Basic Books, February 15, 2005.

4. ADMISSIONS: GATEKEEPERS, DIVERSITY AND AFFIRMATIVE ACTION

American higher education has had a long and somewhat checkered history with respect to access to education. More recently colleges and universities have tried hard to develop policies that attract the best and brightest, yet lend a hand to minorities and other disadvantaged groups that need it. But as always, the devil is in the details.

A giant step toward fairness was taken in June, 2003 following a decision by the US Supreme Court that finally affirmed the constitutionality of affirmative action as applied to college admissions, placing on higher education an indelible mark for generations to come. The decision said that colleges and universities had the right to use race as a factor in their admissions policies, for the purposes of promoting educational diversity, and that this is necessary to create a level field in which race and class in colleges and universities approximate to that of the nation itself.

This landmark decision in the University of Michigan's appeal will be returned to, but first, some background to this long-standing issue of equal access to education.

The events leading to the Supreme Court's decision of 2003 had roots going back to 1992.[13] Then, four white applicants who were rejected by the University of Texas School of Law filed a lawsuit charging that the school's use of different cutoff scores for white and minority applicants violated their right to equal protection under the 14th Amendment. This event triggered a succession of voter initiatives, suits and court appeals. And there was political statesmanship. In 1995 Ward Connerly, a University of California regent, persuaded his fellow board members to bar the University system from using racial, ethnic, or gender preferences in admissions, hiring and contracting. These and many intervening events led to the landmark Michigan decision of the US Supreme Court.

---

13. "Behind the Fight Over Race-Conscious Admissions," in *The Chronicle of Higher Education*, April 4, 2003, pp. A22-25.

Chapter III: Beginnings of the New Transformation

The following is a summary of the history of the dispute over affirmative action:

September 1992: Four white applicants, as just mentioned, are rejected by the University of Texas School of Law. The Center for Individual Rights takes their case the following year.

July 1995: Ward Connerly persuades fellow board members to bar the university system from using racial, ethnic, or gender preferences in admissions, hiring, and contracting.

March 1996: The US Court of Appeals for the Fifth Circuit strikes down the University of Texas Law School's race-conscious admissions policies.

Summer 1996: The Center for Equal Opportunity begins obtaining admissions data from public colleges around the nation. In the ensuing years, it will issue 15 reports covering 56 colleges and will accuse about two-thirds of them of discriminating against white applicants.

November 1996: California voters pass Proposition 209, barring public colleges and other state and local agencies from granting preferences based on race, ethnicity, or gender. Mr. Connerly, the campaign's leader, subsequently announces the formation of the American Civil Rights Institution and its companion political action committee, the American Civil Rights Coalition.

Fall 1997: The Center for Individual Rights files lawsuits challenging admissions policies at the University of Michigan's law school and undergraduate college.

November 1998: Washington State voters pass Initiative 200, banning racial and gender preferences by public colleges and other state agencies.

February 1999: The University of Massachusetts at Amherst stops giving minority applicants an edge in admissions and financial aid decisions, partly in response to the Center for Equal Opportunity's scrutiny.

June 1999: The University of Virginia's president, John T. Casteen III, quietly alters its race-conscious admissions policies, largely in response to scrutiny by the Center for Equal Opportunity and for fear of a lawsuit by the Center for Individual Rights.

November 1999: Seeking to head off a ballot initiative campaign by Mr. Connerly, Governor Jeb Bush of Florida, a Republican, issues an executive order banning state agencies from using preference. Three months later, he persuades the state's university system to cease using race-conscious college admissions.

December 2000: The Center for Individual Rights suffers a setback when the US Court of Appeals for the Ninth Circuit upholds the race-conscious admissions policies formerly used by the University of Washington's law school. The decision is moot in Washington, which remains bound by Initiative 200, but lets six other western states keep race-conscious policies.

April 2002: At the urging of the Center for Equal Opportunity, lawyers from the office of Virginia's attorney general begin advising public colleges throughout the state to curtail race-conscious admissions.

December 2002: The US Supreme Court agrees to hear both Michigan cases.

The decision was focused on a specific case regarding the University of Michigan Law School's policy of accepting students on the basis of a points system. In addition to grades, this case focused directly upon the propriety of using race as a factor when considering applications for admission. As a result of this decision, legal authorities in some states are advising college administrators to use race only for promoting diversity insomuch as it affects a school's educational programs. The decision walked a tight wire in balancing the need to encourage minority students to prepare for professional careers without achieving this aim only by quotas as such. It was deliberately vague so that judgment can be used and applied in particular circumstances. Clearly, there will be no simple litmus test applied to particular cases. Indeed, Justice Sandra Day O'Conner saw this law becoming obsolete perhaps in some 25 years, when inequities have been resolved.

In their decision, the Justices made clear that when parity is achieved naturally by social forces, the government need not continue to audit the admissions records of such institutions, thus releasing colleges and universities from further audits regarding fairness in admissions. In the aftermath of the Supreme Court's decision, it appears that at least some schools are finding enrollment decreasing among undergraduate black and Hispanic admissions.

Efforts to counteract this situation include a small but strong list of institutions that are creating scholarships which were formerly aimed specifically for minority students, but now are being opened up to qualified students of all races and nationalities. In short, it seems that colleges and universities have yet to step up to fully engage the decision. Progress will likely be incremental rather than immediate, and will be influenced by partisan congressional agendas.

Americans pride themselves on being great equalizers of social justice and economic opportunity, personally and through their institutions. But what is preached has not always been practiced. Processes have been perpetuated which result in giving young men and women of economic and social privilege access to top schools in numbers well beyond their proportion in the overall population. Families of means have not only the money but also the connections and know-how to get their offspring into the right colleges and universities. History shows that less than 10 percent of students on the lower rungs of the economic ladder have had access to top-tier institutions.

The new approach appears now to be paying off. As an example, the University of California system, for the first time since it abandoned affirmative action in 1998, has admitted more minority students than it did when it relied on race-based admissions policies.

Indeed, Americans have long practiced racial equality in professional groups like the American Bar Association, the American Medical Association and the American Management Association. Industrial companies, including General Motors, Microsoft, and American Airlines, have for decades explicitly endorsed policies of affirmative action in higher education. The great professional schools of law, business, medicine and others have been successful in bringing more minorities into institutions of higher learning—more than in the case of the arts, sciences and humanities. But the Supreme Court's decision is the first explicit mandate in American higher education for equal access that is coupled with race-based factors. Although less than clear on the issue of public versus private institutions, both forms are likely to be affected for a long time by the outcome of this decision.

What are race-sensitive admissions?[14] William G. Bowen, former President of Princeton and Neil L. Rudenstine, President Emeritus of Harvard, said that "Race-sensitive admissions policies involve much 'picking and choosing' among individual applicants; they need not be mechanical, and are not quota systems, and involve making bets about likely student contributions to campus life and subsequently to the larger society.... We believe that it is morally wrong and historically indefensible to think of race as 'just another' dimension of diversity. It is a critically important dimension, but it is also far more difficult than the others to address." They went on to say that private colleges and universities are as likely as their public counterparts to be affected by the outcome of this debate.

Al Neuharth, founder of USA Today, had this to say in his column of June 27, 2003 headed "Classroom diversity: Race, sex and sense": "The Supreme Court focused attention on the makeup of college classrooms this week when it ruled that sometimes it's O.K. to use race as a consideration in selecting students. That's good. What's *not* good is that too many of us think about race only when it comes to classroom diversity. These are the varied student factors that we actually *should* consider in scoring our schools: race, sex, intelligence levels, financial status, philosophy and geography—and extending to character, personal achievements and leadership qualities." Complex issues require complex metrics.

The rulings on racial preferences in the University of Michigan case will undoubtedly trigger many other modes of affirmative action. Now that schools may not use race as *the* determinant of acceptance, other means will be found to bring minority groups into mainstream higher education. This, obviously, is a good thing. But action encourages reaction, and "minority-only scholarships" are being created to balance racial and ethnic groups further on campuses. Also, the Supreme Court

---

14. "Behind the Fight Over Race-Sensitive Admissions," in *The Chronicle of Higher Education*, Feb. 7, 2003, pp. B7-B10.

was mute as to the administration of financial aid or scholarships, which may open the door to creating minority scholarships for students of every race or ethnic group. After all, deep down, each and every American belongs to some minority group. This unintended consequence of the Court's ruling will undoubtedly be scrutinized by the US Department of Education's Office for Civil Rights.

Another aspect of racial imbalance within academe is the faculties. A 2004 report by a group of Yale University graduate students revealed that even elite universities are still far from achieving parity for faculty members. The report, endorsed by the American Association of University Women, the Feminist Majority Foundation and the Rainbow/PUSH Coalition showed that black and Hispanic faulty members had made virtually no improvement in their careers. Within the Ivy League colleges, new minority PhD recipients were four times more likely to end up in non-tenure-track positions than for white applicants.

Ultimately, all college admissions become personalized: who gets into a particular state-supported college and who does not. In 1997 then Governor George W. Bush signed legislation that automatically admitted into college the top 10 percent of graduates of each high school in Texas. It was hailed as a fair, race-blind solution to achieving greater diversity among the State's incoming college students. But soon after, the Supreme Court ruled that colleges and universities could use some race-conscious criteria in their admissions policies. A wave of alternative proposals followed, aimed at making exceptions for students in low-scoring high schools, and who would otherwise be crowded out by those students from privileged schools. Many educators rightly pointed to the fact that class-rank criteria are poor predictors of college success; there are simply too many other variables at work.

Students who fall within the ten percent overwhelmingly opt to matriculate to the flagship University of Texas at Austin; with rival Texas A&M University the next choice. However, it is quite clear that no single-criterion standard can meet the twin fairness goals of diversity and scholarship. This issue challenges legislators across the country, as they continue to wrestle with a spate of alternative proposals aimed at equity.

An issue closely linked to affirmative action is that of legacy students. It, too, smacks of privilege. Legacy simply means that sons and daughters of wealthy graduates of prominent colleges have a decided edge in getting into those schools. Legacy privilege has long been a factor in public and private schools. At most Ivy League colleges, legacies make up some 10 to 15 percent of students; and they enjoy sharply higher rates of acceptance. This group clearly has an edge and there is currently no nationwide policy to urge more fairness. The marketplace governs.

Princeton and Harvard accept some 35 to 40 percent of their legacy applicants, compared with an 11 percent acceptance rate for the overall national pool. Parents of privilege often expect a kind of *quid pro quo*; if a school admits their child, they will be generous alumni. The issue of legacy practices extends well beyond the upper crust institutions. Financially strapped schools are increasingly looking to attract and graduate students from families with money and influence. These institutions now more frequently accept students from this background, even though some do not measure up academically to their peers. It seems that this practice is becoming more overt. A donation of $20,000 or $50,000 to a favored school, along with transcripts and other supporting information, has a way of securing a student's place in the freshman fall session—even ahead of those who may have better overall credentials.[15]

Students wanting to enter under legacy status should have to meet two criteria. Firstly, do they have the ability to complete the course of study at the institution successfully? And secondly, are the admissions processes and related decisions properly involved with appropriate subjective and non-academic factors? Legacy agreements have generally been seen as appropriate for candidates who are qualified for entrance, as measured against the overall applicant pool. Generally, it is only in marginal circumstances that decisions can be biased in favor of the privileged. Of course, there are cases in which admission criteria are stretched to attract the right applicant, whereby gifts are made to the institution in return for the admission of a son or daughter who might not otherwise be accepted.

---

15. "Buying Your Way into College," *The Wall Street Journal*, March 12, 2003, pp. D1-D2.

In fact, the legacy preference, as it is known, has been nearly as widespread as admissions based on race and ethnicity.[16]

But there are increasing calls to abandon what is seen as a product of class distinction and white advantage. Indeed, several state universities, including Texas A&M, Michigan State and the Universities of Georgia and California, have already officially dropped legacy preferences after having been forced to end racial preference. More state-supported institutions are likely to follow suit soon.

There is yet another wrinkle that enters into the issue of acceptance into college. Harvard and a few other elite schools have revised their rules for early acceptance. These schools no longer allow applicants who apply early, to apply for early acceptance to any other college. Under this new policy, students who have been accepted under the process are not bound to commit to their first choice institution. For these few schools, this policy is really just an "early decision" program. However, the National Association for College Admission Counseling sees it as a violation of their guidelines, which say that students should be free to make multiple early applications, so long as no more that one is binding.

Getting placed in the right college can be very much a game of strategy.[17] Typically, top colleges seek to accept between a third and a half of their prospective entrants into their institution. One reason is that it boosts a college's yield, or the percentage of accepted applicants who decide to attend, a figure that has been a factor in some college rankings, such as published in the annual *U.S. News & World Report* on higher education. Schools like Stanford, Dartmouth and Johns Hopkins now give students who apply early the option to attend other universities of their choice. Harvard and Yale, on the other hand, impose stricter rules for applying early. They require students to submit only one early application, rather than letting them apply early to other schools as well.

---

16. "Preference of Alumni Children in College Admission Draws Fire," in *The Wall Street Journal*, Jan. 15, 2003, p. A1.
17. "The Results Are In on Early Admission" in *The Wall Street Journal*, Jan. 20, 2003, pp. D1-D2.

There are many creative ways for less-affluent parents to position their money so that they look needier than they really are. How? By showing minimized income, by sheltering income or deferring bonuses, and a variety of other financial devices designed to make them look less wealthy than they actually are. Derek Bok, President Emeritus of Harvard, and other leaders have spoken strongly about America's need to do much more to correct the poor practices in preparation for learning afforded by public schools. It is important also that colleges and universities reach out more strongly to work directly with secondary-school educators preparing students for the college experience.

The process of choosing the college or university that is right for the student first entering academe is a real challenge for many. How does one begin? How does one narrow down the field? The choices can be daunting for many: costs and financial aid, reputation, entrance standards, distance/location, etc. But ultimately, most students make their choice on the basis of instinct and peer influence, and not by rational criteria.

Entrance to college can be an intimidating process. College admissions officers are reinterpreting the traditional high school GPA transcript provided by secondary schools. Some high-school administrators simply discard the plus or minus distinctions, feeling such fine distinctions are largely artificial. Others disregard grades from the freshman year of high school, and rely more on class rank. There are many tricks that can be used to put a gloss on reports.

Moreover, many students now are increasingly looking to the Web, not the catalogue, for information on colleges in which they may be interested. And college admissions officers are responding well to this new method of choosing schools. Such schools as the University of Dayton and the University of Kansas are reaching out with new age Web software that can not only inform, but also interact with prospective students. Students can search for particular sectors: humanities, business, technical, ethnic, scholarship, etc., with a view to personalizing education plans. Applications can be submitted easily, and online. And responses can be customized, such as personal invitations for the student and family to visit the campus to meet faculty members. Personal visits to colleges, of course, are always very useful.

Most colleges and universities struggle to maintain high standards for acceptance, while also creating a multi-ethnic student environment. In the case of U.C. Berkeley, the flagship campus of the nine-campus University of California, the admission process also takes note of certain non-academic factors such as special talents or experiences with adversity. They take particular note of underprivileged applicants who have shown such qualities as leadership, community service, and proficiency in the performing arts or athletics. But this approach, too, has its opponents—those who feel that subjective or soft criteria will ultimately dilute the overall quality of the student body. Recent statistics reveal that some 98 percent of California residents who scored above 2,100 (of 2,400 possible) on the SAT examination, and who were seeking places in the highly competitive engineering program, were granted admission to the University of California.

5. THE LEARNING ENVIRONMENT

As a nation, Americans have had many opportunities to enhance the preparation of students seeking college degrees. So, why is it so difficult? The quick answer is that there is an overdependence on practices that were established long ago—almost as far back as the Jefferson era of American history, some two and a half centuries ago. There has been a shift away from the inefficient tutorial system of study inherited from Oxford and Cambridge. And it is now possible for virtually anyone who wants a college education to get one. But there is certainly room for further improvement.

Two of the key issues which still cause problems are relevance and affordability. Richard McCormick, Editor and Publisher of *Manufacturing News*, has said that most universities have been slow to recognize the educational needs of industry and have acted in predictable, self-serving ways to make modest changes to traditional lecture formats. Moreover, he sees colleges and universities as still behaving as if there is no competition from either industry or other colleges and universities. They are largely ignoring the continuous development needs of their graduates, and they cannot see the wisdom of working together on this. It is a prescription for a meltdown of the traditional educational university system.

Others agree.[18] Ronald G. Ehrenberg, Professor of Labor Economics at Cornell University, takes to task the insular and slow-to-act practices that institutions still use. He contends that "colleges are risk-averse and slow to react to market pressures." They tend to follow the salaries of other professions. And there is little, if any, desire for faculty to look for and enact productivity gains. There are no real incentives for faculty and staff to hone their processes and look for efficiencies. Indeed, in the absence of a culture of continual improvement practices, the only response to rising costs is raising tuitions and fees. Extra revenue is needed which, typically, is not being generated through outside sources—except for tuition.

With lifetime learning becoming an integral part of people's lives[19], keeping up with lifelong learning skills via the Internet is essential. *Business Week* reported that, "Doctors often must meet annual educational requirements to prove they are up to date on medical advances. Now, business people find they too must hit the books anew or risk losing out to competitors." In 1984 some 23 million Americans took part in adult education programs. The number topped 100 million in 2004. In 1988 there were just 400 company-run universities; in 1999 it topped 1,600. "And some companies, such as Pensare Inc. of Los Altos, CA, are partnering with the likes of Wharton and Harvard Business School Publishing to develop online programming that corporations can use over their internal networks."

Three of every four MBA students now work full time while pursuing their degree. They need flexibility on the job and at school. Online education is flexible in terms of accessing content at one's convenience. E-mailing assignments, homework, etc., is easy; and the instructors are often able to provide feedback faster than traditional office hours allow.

---

18. "Tuition Rising: Why College Costs So Much," Harvard Press, 2000.
19. "School is Never Out," in *Business Week*, October 4, 1999, pp. 164-168.

For a good blend of face-to-face schooling and Net learning, one model for the future may be Fordham University's Transnational MBA Program. Over a 15-week semester, students meet one weekend a month, usually in or near New York City, but sometimes as far away as Dublin, Ireland. The rest of the time, they communicate with their teachers and fellow students via the Net, reading lectures, filing papers, and doing group work. The students typically work for multinationals such as IBM, and find the school mimics their working day. OnlineLearning.net, the company that develops courseware for UCLA extension, expected its online enrollment to jump from 10,000 in 2000, to about 17,000 in year 2005.

The MBA degree has for decades been the credential of preference for those aspiring to become senior managers. It has been a capstone academic achievement, for it brings together both theory and practice in the areas of economics, marketing, accounting and management. But the luster is beginning to fade in light of criticism from those who see the MBA as being ever more irrelevant because of its stress on theory rather than practical applications as found in real business situations. Warren Bennis and James O'Tool, prominent faculty members at the University of Southern California, call for the redirection of MBA content away from theory and quantitative approaches, and toward building practical business skills and sound ethical judgment.

America has always had its visionary mavericks and those who challenged the status quo, including senior academics. One such is M. Peter McPherson, President of Michigan State University, who pledged that tuition increases would be kept in line with the rate of inflation. It was an unprecedented move away from bureaucratic inflationism and toward fiscal responsibility. That promise has been kept, but not without making changes in the way the university spends its money. He makes note of public institutions' inability to prioritize which, if unchecked, will inevitably lead to non-strategic spending. The result of that is that class sizes continue to increase and faculty salaries languish. Moreover, Pell grants, long a staple for helping students secure their education, no longer cover tuitions and fees as they did earlier. A quarter-century ago, these grants covered some 80 percent of total costs at public four-year colleges; now it is about 40 percent. And pressures will continue to mount as technology-aided learning and instruction will require even more funding. These investments are a big factor that pushes up tuition and fees in the current college climate. This will be covered in Chapter IV.

The largest factor influencing excellence in colleges and universities is money, followed by business strategy to make institutions affordable. State universities have always had difficulty in maintaining program excellence, but now they are finding it daunting. For example, in the mid-eighties the State of Texas funded 49 percent of the budget for its flagship University of Texas at Austin; it is now down to about 20 percent.[20] In the academic year 1966-67 the university had a student-teacher ratio of 15:1; it currently stands at about 19:1.

Comptrollers and related administrators generally do a good job of measuring the financial performance of their institutions, year on year. This is their role and it is clearly of vital importance. So it is with accreditations, the vital set of processes which safeguard the strength of the curricula and the way they are delivered. But it is not sufficient. What is needed is a clear, disciplined approach to measuring continuously the strength of each and all of the components of the institution: programs, students, faculty and staff.

One requirement of an institution is that it operates efficiently and serves the needs of its constituents: students, administrators, faculty and other components, including research programs and stewardship within the community. There is a very powerful concept, taken from the field of mathematics and operations research, which states that in any complex process (productive, legislative, etc.), if you want to achieve optimal performance of the process, you must optimize the system as an entity, and not the individual components. Chapter V.1 has more on this very important principle.

Why is this worthy of consideration? Because it points to how educators can do a better job of educating. If faculty, administrators and staff professionals can work together better, benefits for students (the cus-

---

20. "Greatness Visible," by Paul Burka, *Texas Monthly*, Oct. 2003, pp. 92ff.

tomers) will automatically follow. It is a fact, and one that many corporate universities employ in their courses for tradesmen, sales staff, managers and executives.

Colleges and universities must develop a simple and effective approach to achieving operational improvements. At the heart of this imperative is the need for them to create and enact disciplined systems, including continuing quantitative benchmarks and performance measurements. This philosophy is well embedded in the industrial sector where it has proved to be successful. Such processes for continuing improvement can offer valuable tools for trustees, presidents, administrators and faculty to work together in order to enhance the institution's ability to serve the students and the community.

Some academics have reacted to this by saying that education is different, that they cannot be measured. But specific measurements can and should be developed and used to gage improvements at all levels: institutional, college/department, faculty/staff. These measurements would not be in any sense punitive; on the contrary they would be quite constructive and, if used sensitively, yield real benefits for all parties. The difficulty, of course, is that some people simply do not want to be held accountable for their own performance—and certainly not in a way that allows for comparison with colleagues. But before designing such a process of measurement, there needs to be an understanding of the existing position.

There is a basic flaw in the approach to teaching in that, generally, professors are not taught to teach. It seems self-evident that they should have such training periodically; in what other learned profession are future practitioners not formally prepared for what they do? Faculties argue endlessly about what to teach, but not how it should be taught. There are, of course, many excellent teachers who are fully capable of bringing out the best in each and every student. But the fact is that the vast majority of college professors did not intern in the profession because of a burning missionary calling to teach. On the contrary, the two strongest motivators for scholars to enter the teaching profession are the unstructured lifestyle of professors, and an abiding interest in research.

For many, teaching is simply the obligation they assume in order to secure that lifestyle. Research is important, but it should not be put ahead of teaching.

So, most college teachers have no formal training or preparation at all in the art of teaching. Cornell Thomas, Special Assistant to the Chancellor for Diversity and Community, Texas Christian University, Fort Worth, states that the ability to empower students to think critically about content, beyond the professor's point of view, is seldom enhanced. A process which tries to measure and assess excellence in teaching by using individuals with limited teaching abilities does not work well.

For centuries, intellectual content has been learned through having a teacher standing in front of a passive audience, the communication mostly one way. Of course, some teachers are much better than others in engaging students in discussion and debate, but the scale has always been tipped heavily in favor of the teacher as the conductor.

However, a new approach called problem-based learning (PBL) is rapidly gaining favor, and will likely stand the educational teaching model on its head. This movement is so very important to educating students at all levels as it promises to make everyone better learners. It is no mere fad. PBL can prepare students to be more effective in a world that is changing faster than many can cope with. All educators must and will become familiar with it.

Traditionally, students listened to and took notes from teachers who taught to a prescribed curriculum. Its mantra has been the problem statement, then the analysis and, finally the solution. It used highly structured approaches to understand particular isolated issues: how to solve quadratic equations, how to interpret a Shakespearean play, and suchlike. Two parts fact retention, one part core understanding, this educational approach worked well in a world that was relatively static and changed very slowly over time.

Ben Marcus[21], an Associate Professor at Columbia University, has his students grade his teaching performance, anonymously, because it helps him to assess the clarity of his thinking, his organizational skills

---

21. "Graded by My Students," in *Time Magazine*. January 8, 2001, p. 51.

and the depth of his knowledge. It is an attempt to improve accountability. It also forms a basis upon which tenure is or is not granted, and is a documented dossier that can live forever. "There is, of course, nothing wrong with accountability. But this system assumes that what students need is the same as what they want. Reading my evaluations every semester has taught me otherwise," says Marcus. So he and some of his colleagues have come up with countermeasures. In his field of creative writing—a more subjective field than, say, engineering—students tend to blame the teacher if they get poor marks. He has come up with a deception, one that does not serve to strengthen students' skills but results in higher approval marks. Marcus's deception involves telling the students what they want to hear and praising them, however much they floundered. "And at evaluation time, they would be pleased enough by their 'success' that they would return the praise... I know other teachers who have done the same thing—teaching your heart out to the teachable, but pleasing the unteachable and the disinterested to keep your ratings high."

The world is changing incredibly fast. One way of measuring this acceleration is the "half-life" of knowledge. (This measure borrows from atomic physics, as the time it takes for half of a quantity of radioactive atoms to decay.) Its application to education shows that over time, what has been learned will be replaced by new understanding, tools and technology—which renders irrelevant much of what had been learned earlier. When applied to the value of knowledge accrued in a typical four-year college program, it was found that the half life was about 15-20 years at the turn of the 20th century, but is about 3-10 years now, depending upon the particular discipline. Armed with just the knowledge learned in college, graduates in the future will be required to pursue continuing education throughout their lifetimes just to have the same useful knowledge and competence they had as college students.

This need to keep up is being addressed by posing, analyzing and understanding real problems, not just puzzles. This approach began in the mid-seventies within some medical colleges that understood that students learn and retain more if they approach learning via modules of real world issues. They began to abandon traditional teaching methods whereby students attended lectures, memorized information and took quizzes that generally had right and wrong answers. They began to collaborate with one another rather than compete against each other. School administrators sought to produce physicians prepared as problem solvers and lifelong learners. Medicine, like most professions, has now evolved from recalling facts once learned, to analyzing holistic problems via collaborations between colleagues.

Nowadays, educational technology seems to be mired in yesterday's methods.[22] Too many instructors still rely upon overhead projectors, whiteboards and lectures as their favored educational delivery devices. The lecture format is far from optimal.

> The valuable uses of Information Technology rest upon its ability to provide access to vast information sources, to support discovery-based educational experiences safely, and more aggressively to support peer-to-peer education. In particular, the team-oriented design projects used by many schools, and which I applaud, could be dramatically expanded through the use of simulation and virtual reality. While in the end it is important to get one's hands dirty, the material, cost, and other constraints of doing actual physical fabrication limit the number of such experiences a student can get. Virtual fabrication in a high-fidelity simulated environment can greatly enrich the undergraduate experience.

A teacher of chemistry at the University of Notre Dame,[23] Dr. Dennis Jacobs saw the boredom on the faces of his many students as they shuffled in to his introductory class. Most appeared inattentive and apathetic. So he took the initiative and did something quite different. He recognized that certain "gate-keeping" courses, including introductory chemistry, can be regarded either as an opportunity for students to engage the course, or just as filters that discourage many disinterested students from continued study. What Jacobs did was to add to the course material an extra day of student-led tutorial sessions, required weekly homework, and a more interactive lecture.

---

22. "The Urgency of Engineering Education Reform," by William A. Wulf, The University of Virginia (Past President of the National Academy of Engineering – in The Bent of Tau Beta Pi, Fall), 1998, pp. 21-23.
23. "Precipitating Classroom Change," in *The Chronicle of Higher Education*, May 25, 2001, pp. A12-A14.

Noting that the structure of college science instruction had not changed much since Isaac Newton's time, Jacobs made it modern and relevant. He saw science instruction as a process in which students can actively engage and debate with one another, and the professor, and learn, not just to sit through the course. As an example, he uses sheets of paper, each having a large arrow. He pauses after making a point about, say, the rate of a chemical reaction. Then he will ask whether, under a certain set of circumstances, the rate will be slower, faster, or the same—and why? The students flash their opinions—arrow up for "Yes," down for "No," and sideways for "Don't Know"—and right away Jacobs gets a sense of whether his students are with him or are adrift. He'll ask students to discuss with and explain to their neighbor and defend their answers. The two may agree or disagree but each gets a deeper insight into the issues at hand. Jacobs has found that forcing students to talk to one another about how a problem might be solved gets them thinking about concepts rather than just answers.

This process of active student engagement in understanding answers runs counter to what most instructors are used to. Jacobs finds that the hardest part of his approach is to teaching assistants to refrain from taking over. It is important for the students to have the space to make mistakes and then to recover from them. Does it work? His retention rate in general chemistry increased by 55 percent, and the GPA in his courses has risen dramatically. Slowly, his and other courses that were once thought of as gatekeepers—i.e. intentionally difficult classes that prevented all but the best prepared succeeding—are now becoming training grounds for the next waves of students. It must be working; for his innovation and achievement Dr. Jacobs was named a Carnegie Scholar by the Carnegie Foundation for the Advancement of Teaching.

Today more than 100 law schools are using laptop computers in class.[24] But that makes it easier to cheat and plagiarize. One solution is offered by ExamSoft: test takers get a password, then download an ExamSoft.com program from the company's website. Next, in the exami-

---

24. "ExamSoft Lets Students Take Tests via Laptops", in *The Wall Street Journal*,Dec. 24, 1998.

nation room students are handed diskettes with the test questions. The software keeps them from accessing their computer hard drive and substitutes ExamSoft's simple word processing program. Teachers can set time limits if they choose, either for each question or for the entire test.

Another example that further validates the purpose and value of the problem-based learning concept can be found in one of the key undergraduate courses that engineering and physics students undertake. Statics is the study of the internal forces in bodies and structures that are in equilibrium and is fundamental to the design of all kinds of structures. Traditionally, statics is taught via a few basic principles, and moves from simple to more complex structures. However, more professors are now teaching the subject "upside down." They get their students to use real models of structures to get an overall feel of the internal forces in a structure, and how these forces might change when various imposed loads are applied to it. Baseline studies of student groups who have learned the subject in the traditional manner and those in the new way show clearly that those students learning in the new way have deeper understandings of the course material than those who studied in the conventional way. Clearly, this general approach applies to many other fields of learning.

The basic notion that different people learn differently has yet to be adequately recognized. Individual expressions of learning are encouraged among children, so why not among young and mature adults? The answer may be that it is simply easier to teach in the traditional way.

The ideas and motivation for problem-based learning (PBL) have been nicely articulated by Dr. Stephanie Pace Marshall, President of the prestigious Illinois Mathematics & Science Academy. IMSA is a public residential school for gifted students in grades 10-12. These students are interested in a tough, enriching curriculum. Dr. Marshall sees the migration toward PBL as an evolution which began in the era of Sir Isaac Newton, who regarded the universe as an orderly clock: static, dependable, understandable and predictable. The idea then was that if the components of an issue were understood, they could be assembled into a whole by straightforward intellectual synthesis. Or so it was thought. PBL correctly identifies that the efficient, orderly and linear design of education is no longer useful. In fact, even the human brain does not follow this serial, step-by-step process to problem solving. Rather, it is organic, networked, and redundant; it learns and has efficient pathways to call up and use combinations of information so that people can function. So, if the brain is adaptive, cannot be the approach to learning?

Making the transition from the old to this new paradigm can be a daunting experience, especially for older faculty members who conventionally teach lectures by notes. Yet there are those who have not only made the shift, but thrive in it, and their students queue up to take their courses. There is an emerging market for professional trainers to work with individuals and faculty prepared to seize the opportunity.

The following will further aid understanding of complex natural and social systems. As mentioned, the environment and social structure was regarded in much earlier times as orderly and linear. But various "chaotic" events were also witnessed; unpredictable events that often would reshape worlds: storms, civil rebellions, plagues, earthquakes and tsunamis, drought and other devastating phenomena. But recently, scientists working in such disparate fields as turbulent fluid mechanics, civil uprising and atomic physics have provided a simple yet powerful tool. It turns out that understanding and forecasting such complex phenomena are relatively simple—maybe not in fine detail, but for practical forecasting.

Consider flocks of birds as they fly across the sky. Some flocks are very orderly, such as Canada Geese as they move in near-perfect "V" formations. But most bird flocks fly in seemingly chaotic fashions; part orderly and part randomly. This and other such natural phenomena are regarded as highly random in character. But that is not the case. In his book[25], Mitchell Waldrop shows us how simple a chaotic system really is. Each bird follows a set of three simple rules. It:

---

25. "Complexity: The Emerging Science at the Edge of Order and Chaos," by M. Mitchell Waldrop."

- maintains a minimum distance from birds and other objects in the environment;
- matches its own velocity with that of neighboring birds; and
- moves toward the perceived center of the bird mass.

This model has been simulated on computers many thousands of times, and each and every time birds of a feather indeed form a flock. It seems to be a fundamental principle. From this interesting observation, Waldrop reaches the following conclusions:

- Flocks base their behavior on what each bird does in relation to others, not to what the flock is doing.
- Flocks form from the bottom up, not from the top down (as business organizations do).

The close proximity of birds to their neighbors enables the overall flock to adapt to changing conditions easily and naturally—less turbulence.

And most important, complex behavior, like flocking, need not follow complex rules. A careful look at the rules helps to predict behavior.

Using this flocking model as a paradigm, Dr. Marshall urges a rethink of the assumptions and premises of linear, predictable processes that are managed by persons from above and that are subject to inflexible policies and procedures. By analogy, she makes a plea for a new look to be taken at schools and classrooms, teachers and curricula, and for them to be reconfigured to become the dynamic, adaptive and self-organizing systems they need to be to adapt naturally to new conditions and challenges. A new era is beginning for education, and problem-based learning is a cornerstone of the new paradigm.

How can educational systems be made more effective and efficient? This book urges institutions of higher education to

- make the most of their intellectual and physical assets;
- become more effective and efficient in the way students learn and accomplish;
- provide for life-long learning as a necessity.

But how are these challenges to be approached? What tools should be used? And how is success to be measured in the long term? The issue is not about making higher education in the image of industrial processes.

However, institutions have become locked onto educational systems which are homogeneous, and with which they are unwilling to experiment. Only a very few educational systems stand up and initiate real reform.

The issue is quality in all things, whether in a community college or a Big Ten university. The best template for improving industrial processes is a tool called "Six Sigma." Six Sigma was developed in the mid-eighties at Motorola as a tool for identifying industrial waste and errors, and for correcting them by using the Japanese practice of *kaizen*, or "continual improvement." Despite the distain of some academics, this approach simply is the best general framework for identifying sources of errors and waste in any system. The term Six Sigma derives from a definition of near perfection in any cycle of events; specifically 3.4 errors in a million attempts. It is the best overall framework available for evaluating and improving any well-defined process. It is used in all sectors of manufacturing, health care, and even in managing laboratories and industrial research and development functions. Six Sigma's philosophical approach is aimed at improving process cycle times, reducing errors by better controls, reducing unit costs, and knowing and learning from competitors. It can work in any kind of enterprise which provides services and products, including institutions of higher education.

Approach and intent:

Six Sigma manages the organization's quality agenda by

- setting performance goals for everyone;
- generating sustaining success;
- enhancing value to students (customers);
- accelerating the rate of improvement;
- promoting cooperative learning;
- driving institutional strategic change.

Six Sigma can pinpoint deficiencies in key institutional goals and needs by

- improving lines of integration;
- demolishing barriers to excellence;
- improving leadership and eliminating apathy & discord
- developing crisp, useful and correct goals;
- training everyone in these skills;
- reducing/eliminating cultural and philosophical clashes;

- using revolutionary changes whenever softer approaches are not working.

Understanding and implementing Six Sigma takes skills training and lots of practice. The basic elements include developing useful and quantitative metrics, identifying the processes to be measured, and how. It is also important to understand that Six Sigma is a continuing process not a program. It requires strong leadership and continual reinforcement so that each person is committed to the basic principles and tools. Moreover, the power to change and strengthen these goals resides within local school boards, parent-teacher organizations and trustees; other parents and citizens must also take an interest and get involved.

The most important decision students will make in their young lives is on which college is right for them. There are many factors involved in making that decision: ambition, goals, programs, grades, career choice, and costs. There are also value judgments to be made, such as location, reputation and the perceived "character" of the schools being considered.

In recent years much emphasis had been made on surveys and polls that rank various kinds of community, senior colleges and universities. Two of the most widely read reports on colleges and universities are the *U.S. News & World Report*, and the *Research Doctorate Programs in the United States*, complied by the National Research Council. These summaries are complementary, yet quite different. The US News polls academics and ranks undergraduate and graduate programs by various standard criteria. Because these annual rankings are so visible to the public, institutions pay great attention to strategies that might increase certain of these metrics so that they will poll higher in the future. The NRC reports, compiled every ten years, address graduate programs in a wide range of fields. In both these polls, it is difficult to climb up the ladder quickly, as competitors are also striving for improvement.

In the race to the top, all colleges and universities scramble to find ways to gain higher rankings. But it is increasingly difficult, particularly among strapped, state-funded colleges and universities. What is clear is that the surest way to achieve higher ratings is for faculties to continually improve their teaching/coaching performance and offer their students the best possible educational experience so as to instill loyalty and support throughout their careers. Today's graduate is tomorrow's donor.

The K-12 educational sector is also beginning to make real strides in providing improved educational processes. It simply is not true that the best way to evaluate students in any discipline is through essays (which are increasingly plagiarized, anyway). There are better, more effective learning tools available, if used properly.

Students, parents, legislators and taxpayers expect more from the education system. Those working in education could learn from the industrial sector and its fight to stay ahead in tough, international markets in bringing products and services to consumers. If it had not heeded the warning in the early eighties—that its international competitors were getting better and smarter—the economy certainly would not be as strong as it is today. How was this achieved? By eliminating mindless chores and replacing them with appropriate automation; by upgrading automation tools; and by ending work-in-process inspections. If the process was right, and the automation was regularly inspected and calibrated, the outcomes would, in consequence, be the best possible. This simple model should be in the mind of every faculty and staff member, as well as academic and staff administrators. There is a duty of care to the student customer. Upholding this will result both in better student learning and reduction in the cost of education.

Is it true that learning is somehow inversely correlated with classroom size? The answer, happily, is no. Rather, the focus should be on two more vital imperatives. Firstly, good teachers can be taught to be excellent ones. This demands that faculty members must regularly participate in (not just attend) sessions on how to be even better teachers. This is happening at the University of Iowa and others across the United States, and is in the spirit of the process of continuing improvement, mentioned earlier.

Secondly, there is a need for more teamwork and more cooperative learning. Students really need to know how to do both, for these social skills will be valuable in their after-college years. The following are some guidelines.[26]

- Require students to take study-skills courses or to attend orientation sessions that emphasize time management.
- Involve faculty members in campus gathering tours for prospective freshmen, to emphasize the importance of academics.
- Provide rewards to faculty members who pay extra attention to their teaching and time with undergraduates.
- Create learning communities in which students work in groups with faculty and staff to develop classes that will create a better sense of connection to the university and to academic work.

The way in which courses are scheduled needs to be examined. Most institutions offer courses on the semester basis (i.e. two sessions per academic year), although some still use the quarter system (three per academic year, excluding summer sessions). The quarter system provides for more individual courses, and more choices—at the sacrifice course time. Either way, the (false) assumption is that all courses have equal intellectual content and scope. This "one size fits all" concept has to go; and if a particular course has greater scope, then it should be scheduled into two semesters. There also needs to be improvement in courses according to the content needed. It is more complex administratively but there can and should be scope for "mini" courses which would give students exposure to some topics that, once introduced, are understood quickly. Examples include ethics in business, communications, and other "soft" topics where students need at least an exposure to the subject.

This is starting to happen at institutions such as the Massachusetts Institute of Technology (MIT) and Northwestern University (NU). MIT's Sloan School of Management has overhauled their MBA, splitting its traditional 13-week semester into two six-week sessions with a week of reflection in between. This affords the students an opportunity to get together informally with faculty research and on interesting and relevant topics. Courses which require a traditional semester (or quarter) can be accommodated by scheduling back-to-back sessions. NU's Master of Product Development program works on a similar principle, but holds to the quarter system. In this program all but two courses (of a total of 22) are full-quarter in length; all others are half-quarters. The result is that

---

26. "Homework? What Homework?" *The Chronicle of Higher Education*, Dec.6, 2002, p. 36-37.

students have a much broader scope, in a way that allows them to pick up quickly.

There is enormous opportunity for colleges and universities to make disruptive and improved changes in the processes used to serve students. They have been bound by tradition in many ways—like the semester (or quarter) calendars with all but vacant academic programs during summers—and little is being done to provide useful adult continuing education, for fun or for profit. As a result, other providers are filling the vacuum, with the institutions becoming marginalized.

Who are the opportunists? Beginning in the 1980s, a network of some 3,500 corporate universities has been established to provide continuing professional education for working adults needing better skills, from accounting to zoology. By and large, they have been quite successful and vital to the nation's competitiveness. Consider also the burgeoning business of for-profit colleges and universities that have ushered in a new era of continuing education. Traditional institutions have failed to take ownership of this opportunity, thereby missing the chance to become an eager and more aggressive competitor.

Undoubtedly, the American system of higher education is still the best in the world, despite its many flaws. The need is for continuing innovation and the abandonment of outmoded practices. Colleges and universities must change and charge ahead into the future. They must develop a form of distributed leadership in which faculty and administrators no longer work in isolation but in cooperation. They must continue to hone their tools of intellectual leadership, learn just how to learn and keep up in a changing world, and about better teamwork and continuing enhancement of teaching skills. The business sector has proved that this works and pays off; to do less is simply to squander the future.

6. Pedagogy: Trends and Measuring Educational Outcomes

Students today are generally spending less time studying than they used to. The rule of thumb is still at least two hours of class preparation for every hour spent in the classroom; or 25-30 hours a week. However, for many reasons students do not come near to meeting that target. This is especially true of many college freshmen, who tend to do less outside-class preparation. Many of them see college as simply an extension of high school. Without intervention, many will fail. Only half of the grades given at Harvard College and peer institutions are As. The main excuse—or justification—is that there is increasing competition and more content to master.

Educators must take a serious look at the phenomenon of grade inflation and its consequences. This is a national trend that has accelerated in the past two decades. A century ago, a C was awarded for average work; roughly the medium grade in a typical class. This is no longer the case. Grades have crept up to the point where a C is regarded as borderline failure.

There are two appropriate and central questions to be asked: Why? And does it matter? Regarding the former, there are more collateral materials available that students can easily access, including in the form of papers, essays, etc., for assignments and homework. At its worst, there is a huge, web-accessible, black market for plagiarism. It is wrong, of course, but tempting. Secondly, larger classes of students make it more difficult for teachers to get to know them on a personal basis. Yet another aspect is societal: more college students are made to take remedial courses as freshmen and sophomores. Students have always found ways to inflate their grades, as it is in their interest when seeking employment. Grade inflation appears to be a real problem without any solution.

In preparation for seeking admission to the college, several millions of high school juniors and seniors each year prepare for, and take the dreaded American Council on Education (ACE) (Iowa City) or the Scholastic Assessment Test (SAT) (New York) board examinations. Most students make their own study arrangements, although there are several independent companies such as Kaplan Test Preparations and Triumph College Admissions which coach students in readiness for these particular tests. The two standardized tests generally do a good job in evaluating students' preparation in the key areas of English grammar and reading comprehension, general and advanced mathematics and science and, usually, personal essays about their passions and accomplishments. The purpose of these tests is to predict how well students will fare in doing college-level work. They do this quite well.

Yet standardized testing has its own drawbacks. The University of California's President, Richard C. Atkinson, sounded a shrill alarm when, in 2002, he dropped the SAT I examination requirement for entrance into the Cal system. This is the traditional two-part verbal and math examination, taken by some two million high school students every year. Certainly, some part of his decision was based upon the awareness that no test can be fair and impartial to all students. Test takers represent a wide variety of abilities, and some are clearly handicapped by circumstances over which they have little control: language, economic level, quality of teachers, desire to achieve and other factors. The new standard, SAT II, is wider in scope and consists of critical reading, math and writing; the former standard portion on analogies has now gone.

The overall goal of such testing, of course, is for all students entering college to have a background sufficient to be capable of completing an associate or baccalaureate degree. The reality, however, is that about 25 percent of college freshmen drop out by the end of their first year; and only 50 percent graduate within five years.

Society believes that it has gone a long way to realizing true egalitarianism among students across America. But has it really? It is clear that students graduating from selective or prestigious colleges are more likely to enjoy privileges and opportunities than those who do not. Despite all the attention and rhetoric about equal access to education, there is still some way to go. There are scores of studies which conclude that students of economic and intellectual privilege will outperform colleagues who lack such privilege. And no one disputes that being launched from well-branded schools offers lifetime benefits in terms of income and social access.

Colleges and universities are much more sensitive to these issues than before. The University of California abandoned affirmative action in 1998, and now admits more minority students that it did earlier, when it used race-based criteria for admissions. Ward Connerly, regent of the

University of California system, says that high school students no longer need any special treatment to gain entry to the UC system; only to work hard and have confidence in themselves. This mind-set is fast settling into admissions officers at colleges and universities across the US.

Yet the bottom line is still that those youths who attend private and selective schools during their early education have a huge advantage in gaining admittance to the right college. A study reported in *The Chronicle of Higher Education*[27] showed that of the 50 wealthiest institutions by endowment, 35 (70 percent) were private. And it is no surprise that faculty members in these institutions tend to have more resources and are often better teachers in the sense that they can spend more time giving individual attention to students, and developing better visions of what they want in the future.

---

27. "Class Rules: The Fiction of Egalitarian Higher Education," in *The Chrcnicle of Higher Education*, July 25, 2003, pp. B7-10.

Chapter IV: Technology's Transformational Role in Higher Education

Systems that are Needed to Take Us into the Future

Topical Themes
1. Forces of Change: Demographics Accelerating Knowledge
2. Technology: Conventional, Distance and Internet-based Learning
3. Business Information & Library Systems
4. Managing and Reining in Technology Costs
5. Benchmarking
6. Intellectual Property

1. Forces of Change: Demographics and Accelerating Knowledge

When it comes to educating students, most colleges and universities are still stuck in the dark ages. In ancient Greek times, and for centuries thereafter, knowledge was rare, and thirsty minds sat at the feet of masters, eager to soak up ideas, facts and frameworks. Students were then handpicked by station and passion for education; most were excluded. Modern society encourages, even *requires* that all people become knowledgeable learners. The irony is that despite all the advances in knowledge and technology, students by and large are still learning in much the same way as their ancient forebears. Today's environment offers abundant opportunity for all colleges and universities that can envision a better future, if they are bold enough to seize it.

This section deals with issues regarding global demographics and how they will affect learning institutions. There are enormous worldwide patterns of change underway that will affect all higher education. The populations of the world's advanced nations, for the first time in recorded history, are now shrinking. (India is the notable exception.) If current birth rates continue, the population of Italy will shrink by about two-thirds before the end of this century; Japan's population will be about half in the same period. The United States is still growing, but its population will peak in about 2015, after which it will begin to taper off. A decline in the number of 18- to 22-year old students, the conventional market for higher education, can be anticipated.

Jack Forstadt is a visionary regarding future work and educational patterns. Some of his notions of the changing workspace in the decades ahead are given below.

- For the first time in world history, by the year 2015, smaller populations will start to be seen in most nations with the exception of India. By the end of this century there will be declines in Europe of some 50 percent.
- Advanced nations will move from a system of capital and manual labor, to one that fosters knowledge workers. Emerging nations will take on more of the world's manufacturing.
- Productivity will increase as health care and standards of workplace safety get ever better. People will work longer before retirement, and will work for more, and different, organizations than ever before.
- There will be fewer students in the 18-22 age range. Choice and flexibility will mark a fundamental change as to how higher education is pursued. The emergence of for-profit colleges and universities is a precursor to this trend and will set the pace for the future.
- For traditional colleges and universities to continue to operate as they have, they will need to reinvent themselves continually by finding ways to cut costs and become more efficient in their operations.
- Colleges and universities will become leaner, more efficient and effective in how they dispense knowledge to students. Teachers will teach more courses and hours. They will increasingly use a variety of educational technologies to make learning more enjoyable and effective.

- Because of the shrinking demographics and diminishing numbers of conventional colleges/universities, there will be changes in their missions. They will open their doors 12 months a year, and will enroll students of all ages. Tenure will change and wane in importance.
- Corporations will continue to exert more influence in the arena of continuing education. They will wield more power regarding what is taught in degree programs.
- Technology can and will forever change the way people learn. Any holdups in its advance will come from anti-technology Luddites who will continue to shy away from any new methods and ideas that they fear.

People learn most of what they need to function through various combinations of intelligence models, such as logic, spatial awareness, language, analysis, music and inter/intrapersonal skills. No one is gifted in all of these dimensions. But in all learning, be it sports, dancing, cooking, physics, social etiquette, and so forth, people learn by using the tools that suit them best. Some may learn by reading, others by discussion, still others by experimenting with physical models. Individuals use their strongest talents as they learn.

But that is *not* the case with conventional higher education. For the most part, students take their seats, listen attentively and passively take notes. Some of the brightest and most gifted people were poor students, simply because the model used in higher education is one-dimensional. Students are talked to and they absorb what they can. For most, this is not a good approach for learning. Learning at its best is communal and interactive. To paraphrase Henry Ford, the idea is that "you can have any education you want as long as it's delivered by lecture." This approach clearly is waning today.

There needs to be a different approach, and the learning process must be modernized. As an example, product and service industries are catching onto the notion of mass customization. This term refers to situations in which vendors will tailor their products and services to the particular needs and desires of their customers. It may still be the same wireless telephone, pair of eyeglasses or stock portfolio, but it has been specifically crafted to fit the consumer's particular style and preferences. Consumers now expect this level of service in much of what they purchase and eventually higher education will provide this kind of service to everyone.

It is interesting to consider just why there are such huge differences between industrial companies. Size certainly is not a measure of excellence; companies of all sizes and ages emerge and disappear every day. As a nation, the US economy thrived on production processes. The need to give value led to improvements and efficiencies. And now a new era of mass customization is underway. Yet by contrast, higher education has seen precious little process improvement. Little has changed fundamentally in the practice of pedagogy over the past two and a half millennia. The wise and learned have stood before their young apprentices, teaching them. Is there any other professional field that has such a poor history of advancing its art and craft?

Educators should be all about delivering great quality to their customers, containing costs, working smarter, having a clear and executing a well-drawn vision. And why are there not much larger differences between higher education institutions? Of course, there are differences between them with respect to size, endowments, reputations, entrance requirements, sports programs. But these markers are largely irrelevant to student-customers. For them, it is all about quality and value.

Higher education can improve. There are those who do not like the term "customers" being used to describe students, but that is exactly what they are. The role of educators should be to serve them in the best possible way. The Henry Ford approach simply will not be acceptable in the years ahead. The free market of ideas and innovation will take care of that. And those academics still clinging to the one-dimensional, traditional delivery of education will be looking for alternative careers.

Fortunately, some very attractive educational innovations are being introduced. Leading educators are experimenting—usually successfully—with a mix of delivery modes: teamwork, online content, simulations and, indeed, traditional lecture formats. It is a step toward mass customization in education, as evidenced in the Olin College of Engineering in Needham, MA, and others, where students are expected to be partners with their faculty in finding ever better patterns of learning.

This carries the promise to make education much more responsive to individual student needs. The transition from traditional to customized learning will be fascinating to observe.

As an example, there is a revolution coming in the way science and engineering is taught. Virtual lab experiments are beginning to displace traditional experimentation methods; they are faster, safer, and less expensive. A virtual chemistry lab allows students to complete assignments and submit their results online. Because of the speed, students can experiment faster with various doses and mixtures, temperatures and times, and get a better feel for the science behind the exercise—without causing an explosion. It is more entertaining and less stressful. The same applies to physics, biology and other sectors of science. These virtual teaching tools can help students get a greater grasp of the purpose of the experiments, and the sensitivity of the outcomes when introducing different initial conditions. Moreover, virtual labs can be of enormous benefit to distance learning students. Continued experimentation with the art and science of education is vital. In this era of continual change, everyone must strive for improvement, whatever the field of learning.

What does the future hold for higher education, in terms of demand? The Baby Boomer age is nearing its end. This demographic phenomenon refers to the surge of births roughly between 1945 and 1965. As a group, these citizens are now affluent and have children of their own entering college. The capacity to educate them will be tested. This bump in demographics will last for another decade or so, after which it will begin to go down. But for colleges and universities, some forecasters are betting on a protracted period *beyond* the bump, bolstered by first-generation minority groups that aspire for their slice of American pie.

Below are the statistics for US citizens of all age groups, taken from the US Census Bureau for the year 2000—the total is just over 281 million.

These data show a primary swelling in the group of American Baby Boomers that, at the crest, averages some 22 million people within a 5-year sector. Following this group is the current generation of their progeny, a secondary bump which peaks at about 20.4 million Americans within that 5-year sector. The trough between these two peaks includes about 19.8 million Americans in their 5-year group. Doing the mathematics, this suggests that the Boomer Progeny group will produce a bulge of about 10 percent more college-age men and women, cresting in about 2008. Also, behind the second bubble there is little reduction in numbers. Basically, the demand for conventional college and university slots will be stronger than ever, and for as far as can be seen into the future.

Table 4.1 Number of Americans by Age Group

Age Group	Number in Millions
<5	19.177
5-9	20.549
10-14	20.527*
15-19	20.220
20-24	18.994
25-29	19.382
30-34	20.325
35-39	22.797
40-44	22.443**
45-49	20.092
50-54	17.585
55-59	13.424
60-64	10.704
65-69	9.534
70-74	8.859
75-79	7.416
80-84	4.945
85+	4.241

*Progeny of "Baby Boomers"
**Generation of "Baby Boomers"

America is becoming a nation of telecommuters, working by use of an electronic linkup with a central office.[28] Some 24 million adults in the US regularly or occasionally telecommute. "...Companies now generally allow only proven performers to telecommute. But not so for our newcomers, a group which feels entitled to have flex-time. This makes for a pattern that can lead to resentment among co-workers towards telecommuters, who then feel as outsiders; they cannot be at impromptu

---

28. *Wall Street Journal* of October 31, 2000, pp.B1 ff.

meetings. The fact is that it is harder to be a team of one. People need eyeball contact if they're to work together effectively. Many companies have been dabbling in telecommuting with a structure, and run like scared rabbits when it doesn't work out," says Kay Morgan, a vice president at Management Recruiters International, Inc. Some large companies, including AT&T, can offer some of their employees a day-a-week of telecommuting. Others favor taking that day not as a standing day, but rather at the pleasure of the supervisor. A key factor in effective telecommuting is trust. But that leads to picking and choosing who can, and cannot telecommute.

2. TECHNOLOGY: CONVENTIONAL, DISTANCE AND INTERNET-BASED LEARNING

Some of the elements of modern learning are self-study, learning from a professor, and learning from other students.

Internet-based asynchronous education has the promise of providing all three of these elements, in any combination. It has two distinguishing features that apply to higher education. Firstly, it is an extremely efficient mechanism for the distribution of educational materials. And secondly, it enhances communication between learner and professor, and between learners themselves.

Learning can be divided into three distinct approaches. First is *traditional*, the in-class, schoolroom environment. Second is *passive*: With this, the student reads and is tested periodically throughout the course of study. It is well-suited for training and for non-credit short courses. The third model is *active*, the broadcast or online publishing model. Here, the focus is on degree-seeking students, many of whom are employed and want to upgrade their skill sets via the Internet.

Despite all the hype about the impact of these non-traditional learning approaches, universities, colleges and community colleges remain the dominant providers of for-credit education, accounting for more than 95 percent of the million or so online enrollments. Among the largest of these are the University of Maryland University College (UMUC), and the State University of New York (SUNY). Among the for-profits, the University of Phoenix is the largest, though still behind UMUC and SUNY in enrollments. In the engineering disciplines, Stanford University, the Georgia Institute of Technology, the University of Washington and the University of Illinois (Urbana-Champaign) are among the leaders. All provide Masters Degree programs online.

The internet is also a very efficient distributor of materials. It provides a communication mechanism for promoting and enhancing interaction between the learner, the learner community and the professor and is highly interactive. Asynchronous Learning Network (ALN) is now in for-credit, degree-oriented education. Costs are relatively small for creating a course in this model, between $5,000 and $15,000. Over time, the cost of this interactive net mode of learning will drop down to about the same as creating a traditional on-campus course, while the cost of delivery will be about 20 percent below that of the campus course.

Frank Mayadas, Program Director of the Sloan Foundation, believes that within five to ten years all courses for traditional on-campus students will involve some kind of web element (e.g. assignments, including syllabus; discussions, tutoring) to complement the traditional classroom. Already, around half of all courses offer this. Adult learners who live near campuses will have the option to take evening classes as they do now, or to take classes through a hybrid approach, such as coming in for an evening class once a week, and doing the rest online. Some students will do this, while others will opt to do much or all of their work online. The opportunity to mix and match will be available for these learners.

Only a small fraction of new knowledge is created in academia. Most of it comes from the environments of manufacturing and new product development, banking, or retail, to give a few examples. In the traditional educational paradigm, it is difficult to bring this newly created knowledge directly to the learner, other than in a delayed fashion by way of books. But online education makes it possible to bring industry experts into a virtual classroom, as a guest lecturer.

Mayadas points to another feature of internet-based learning—the ability to muster peers to help a student that is stuck on a problem. Help can be there almost instantaneously. This is more that just being time efficient; it actually enhances learning. ALN technology also affords terrific opportunities for continuing learning and skills improvement. It will, quite literally, improve the nation's standard of living.

Despite what may be read in the press, there is a growing awareness in traditional universities and colleges of the impact of non-traditional learning. Clearly, the most powerful new movement in higher education today is technology-aided learning. It has affected and molded the way we learn, and will continue to do so. And as with all disruptive social movements, those who ignore or fail to properly assess these events will be left behind.

There are two dimensions in this educational movement. Firstly, manufacturers such as Ford Motors and Cisco Systems have arranged online courses to train their employees better and faster. The virtual classroom is an easy way to brief sales forces on the latest products, or to teach the mechanics of new auto engines. This movement will grow and have an enormous impact on the training of entire workforces.

The second dimension is in the field of higher education. Here, two revolutionary forces are invading campuses: the explosion of for-profit teaching enterprises, and the widening use of technology-aided instruction. Both use technology, but in different ways. The for-profit enterprise wave developed in large part because traditional colleges and universities failed to see it or the need for it. They had grown accustomed to delivering college and professional education in the old-fashioned way.

For-profits must follow rigorous Federal standards of legitimacy for them to operate. Although these colleges are eligible for Federal grant and loan funding, the for-profit sector still suffers from the lack of adequate access to the wide array of Federal programs and financial aid that mainstream, not-for-profit institutions enjoy.

The focus is still on students in the key 18-25 group who move to campuses, study for about 75 percent of each calendar year, learn mostly passively from teachers delivering lectures, and typically end academic exposure when they have finished their degrees. The college experience is a great way to prepare for the real world, but little is done to educate men and women beyond their graduation. They will continually need fresh knowledge and information, but the provision of lifetime education has largely defaulted to other education providers in the private sector.

There is another element of conventional higher education that is seldom addressed: the preparation of students for employment. Culturally, the move from campus to office is often an overnight transition. It is overwhelming for many graduates and academics do not deal with it very well. It is fraught with hidden traps and missteps. The change from gown to suit should be shared by both sides, to make the transition as smooth as possible.

Employers hiring graduates usually provide some form of induction, information about the company and its culture, and the role and expected contribution of the graduate. Often this is done informally, but increasingly the trend is toward formal induction sessions to help new employees settle in as quickly at possible, which is mutually beneficial. Whereas employers generally do a good job at welcoming and orienting the new starts, colleges and universities, by contrast, are generally poor at preparing students for the move. So it seems reasonable that faculties should take on a part of this responsibility, but few do. Most professors lack the experience, interest, insight or ability to counsel their graduates effectively about how to take this major step from college graduate to working professional. This simple step would be a giant one when releasing graduates into the workplace, before they sign the employment contract.

A look will now be taken at the new competitors in the arena of academia, the for-profit institutions. At the top of the list, by sheer volume of enrollments, is the University of Phoenix (UOP), a giant that offers both online and in-class educational formats around the clock. It is the nation's largest private university, with 35 campuses in major cities across the US and has an enrollment of about 160,000 students, about 65,000 of who study online at home or in the office. Their enrollment is far greater than any traditional university in the US. The UOP engages some 9,000 experienced faculty, 250 of who are full time. Its market tends toward mature students; the average age is 35. Tuition averages about $10,000 a year, about 55 percent of what a typical private college charges. A key factor is that UOP does not have such infrastructures as student unions, sports teams, and student societies. But it makes money.

For-profit educational enterprises like the University of Phoenix generally employ part-time faculty members who are also working professionals in their fields. Content experts quality control the content of the faculty members intend to deliver. Phoenix has a strong administration just for this situation.

These institutions tend to focus more on classroom performance than do traditional college professors, who generally have not had any formal coaching in the art. For example, instructors at UOP must have five years of recent professional teaching experience, a master's or doctorate degree, and must undergo a month of unpaid training in teaching. This, together with better-focused students and tuitions and fees which are as little as one-third those at leading private institutions, makes a compelling case for their future success.

Table 4.2 Major For-Profit Education Providers[29]

	Assoc	Bachelor	Master	Doctorate
Apollo Group (inc. UOP)	1	12	27	4
Capella University	-	2	6	4
Career Education	86	29	9	2
Corinthian Colleges	23	10	2	0
DeVry, Inc.	2	7	7	2
Education Management	25	21	23	13
ITT Educational Services	6	8	1	0
Jones International University	0	4	4	0
Strayer Education	10	8	6	0
Sylvan Learning Systems	0	2	23	12

DeVry, Inc. is another major player in the for-profit college market. It was founded in 1983 and now operates as a part-time-undergraduate college system. It currently runs more than 20 undergraduate campuses, with 80,000 students, across the US. It also owns the Keller Graduate School of Management, which has some 40 major facilities and 300 smaller rented sites for its Becker Conviser CPA Review programs. Keller

---

29. The Chronicle Index of For-Profit Higher Education, August 15, 2003, p. A28.

went public in 1991. DeVry, Inc. has a 70-year history of classroom education and is venturing onto the Web. Its Keller organization has been offering classes online since 1998 and launched its BS in business administration in 2001.

Maybe this is why DeVry and other new age college forms are so successful. Their faculties have worked together and focused on processes and outcomes, not just on routine packaged course content. Their students tend to be more determined to succeed. There are no research studies to attend to and no faculty committees to drain away time. It is pure, undiluted education, and they are successful at it.

Of course, not all students and teachers agree that the Internet is *the* answer to the problems of higher education. Many say that the internet may create some new problems ahead. There is a growing backlash from teachers and parents who question the very use of computers in classrooms. With students distracted by technology and understaffed schools unable to maintain costly infrastructures, computers often just clutter classrooms, leaving critics to question whether the money could be better spent elsewhere. And in universities, including those among the top tier, educators are also taking a cautions approach as professors battle with administrators over intellectual property rights, and debate whether technology might forever change higher education as they know it. Some fear the diminution of their ranks and reduction of academics to mere knowledge workers who produce information for profit. These skeptics point out that at least two high-profile ventures, Western Governors University and California Virtual University, have already failed in their efforts.

This is a volatile industry. In 2003, a new online university, Universitas 21, was launched with the vision of serving students living in developing countries. This consortium of 17 research universities in ten countries (including one American, the University of Virginia) began operations with an MBA program. There are no live lectures in this institution; students work at their own speed and convenience. And in 2002, Sylvan shed its elementary and secondary facilities to focus instead on online education and its network of international universities. Sylvan intends to build a post-secondary education company serving 200,000 students. It already has campuses in Chile, France, Mexico, Spain and Switzerland.

The market for for-profit degree programs will continue to grow rapidly. There is a thirst for nontraditional students to take advantage of good, affordable college programs geared to their individual needs and paces. Also, the fact is that this new approach to higher education is not entirely incremental. That is, these new wave colleges are taking away some of the traditional market's share. It is yet another wake-up call for traditional colleges and universities to re-think fundamentally their role in holistic education, and go beyond the traditional student cohort in their approach to learning.

Finally, for-profit educational enterprises have won their war for respectability.[30] There now are 41 regionally and professionally accredited business schools, 89 regionally accredited schools of education and 51 regionally accredited schools of engineering. They charge fees on a per-credit-hour basis, a range from as low as $100 to $1,000. Most of the newcomers offer programs through mainstream colleges and university sites. All but about a dozen states now have online graduate programs. Location means little in cyberspace.

If schools like the University of Phoenix and DeVry are so good, what are the downsides of this mode of approach to higher education? First, of course, is the socialization element which pulls young students into the college experience. It is a powerful and important aspect of the traditional higher education process. It provides an environment that creates growth, real friendships and camaraderie. But this dimension is much weaker among students going to traditional colleges. This distinction is a subtle, but powerful force in the education process. Another weakness of this new approach to college can be a lack of interaction between students and professors. Some students feel so isolated that they simply drop out. Yet another is the issue of academic integrity: there may be no proper assurance that the real student takes the exams.

---

30. *The U.S. News and World Report*, Oct. 28, 2002, pp. 64-68.

Some of these deficiencies are being bolstered by various kinds of institutional branding. Students can now supplement their online courses with their own customized screen formats, and can even receive lectures from cyberspace given in the actual voices of the professors. Strayer University Online, for example, has hired professional readers to record faculty members' lectures for audio playback. The aim is to guarantee that all online lectures meet the university's quality standards for clear delivery. The drawback of this is the loss of live discussion between instructors and their students.

MIT has now adopted a bold approach to online education. Former President Charles Vest and his faculty are absolutely convinced that open software systems are the way forward. They believe that general knowledge should be *free*. The Internet is a fundamental tool for learning and, hence, MIT should and is giving away its teaching materials. This great institution is making many of its courses freely available to everyone interested, under the premise that online course content is inexpensive to produce, and it services the greater objective of creating a more enlightened society.

MIT officials have now created a website,[31] "OpenCourseWare," at ocw.mit.edu, which will expand access to educational materials, making some 2,000 MIT course materials available free and without restriction to the public for noncommercial use by 2007. Faculty members everywhere will be able to "cut and paste" content segments to create new courses with special twists and accents. A growing number of schools are participating in this project, including Carnegie Mellon, Foothill-DeAnza Community College, George Mason University, Harvard University, Johns Hopkins, Tufts, the University of Michigan, the University of Texas and Utah State University, and others have similar plans to participate. The overall message here is that, for the first time ever, formal intellectual knowledge is emerging as a free right for all citizens.

Before the 1980s and 90s, when professors began to be more sensitive to copyright issues in making up their course materials and lectures, educators generally regarded teaching materials as fair use. Anyone

---

31. "MIT's Open Window," *The Chronicle of Higher Education*, Dec. 6, 2002, pp. A32-33.

could use them as they wished. For the most part, this understanding is still in play; course materials are seen as consumables that have short half-lifes and not owned property. Courseware is seen as ever-evolving and ever more rapidly. The advantage that schools see is not so much the content, which is relatively conventional, but rather how effective the professor is at teaching and instilling the principles and applications. Frank Mayadas, the program director at the Alfred P. Sloan Foundation, puts it in perspective: "Regardless of the motivation and desire, this movement isn't going to take off like wildfire—because of the costs involved."

In a related movement, there is also a trend toward free, open-source software, spearheaded by Linux. In line with this movement, Jones Knowledge, Inc., which consists of more than 100 online colleges, and their Jones e-Global Library, gives away the source code for their popular course-management system, "e-Education." Their market strategy is to focus exclusively upon their core business of delivering higher education. This is in step with their organizational goal to democratize higher education via the Internet. Providing their CMS system free to developing countries gives them an entry into international colleges and universities that may not have the resources to use and maintain sophisticated software. Only time will tell whether user institutions will be capable of adapting and keeping current source code that is not centrally supported.

However, as in any new enterprise, there are winners and losers. New York University and Temple University have had to shut down their for-profit online educational programs for financial reasons. And some others are also struggling. At the core of the difficulties is the fact that there still is a great deal of confusion in the marketplace. The largest audience today for non-traditional higher education is made up of working adults who must keep their current jobs. They require convenience and good student services, such as communication with their professors and student groups, academic advice, and financial and career counseling. These needs seem better served by the for-profits.

Another factor is that prospective students are now confronted with a huge array of choices. They struggle with distinguishing between e-learning and for-profit offerings and other programs delivered on-line from traditional colleges and universities. The market for non-paced, online programs is becoming more crowded and branding and price will be the strongest determinants of success. Pricing of programs is important, especially for start-up, online institutions. Universitas 21 and similar private online universities must create new cost strategies that can even out the currencies and economic levels of regions and countries in which such programs are given. Traditional colleges and universities are beginning to crowd into the online marketplace, and may have an advantage over competitors.

Among the major Internet learning institutions are SmartForce, which supplies companies with their web platform content and management systems for online training; Docent, which provides internet infrastructure for companies using web-based learning; and the Varsity Group, which operates an online textbook retail operation that provides college marketing services. DeVry also offers online and classroom-based courses to a wide array of industries.

The promise of e-learning is that students can connect with their instructors via the Internet. Students must be able to download materials and content, such as video and audio lectures, and participate in class discussion remotely. They can talk with their instructors online, and can socialize and collaborate with their peers through chat rooms and message boards. Professors and students alike can view materials for conducting research for class or projects. They often place more trust in published print media than online information sources. Some schools carry this environment all the way to fulfillment and completion of degrees, all online.

E-learning is now online and flourishing at Harvard, Brown, MIT, Stanford and other elite schools. They have long argued that there is no substitute for the small and precious things students learn from their residential experience: meeting informally with professors, socializing with peers and otherwise soaking up the academic culture. Some alumni and students fear that credit given for Web courses could dilute schools' highly cultivated brand names. But these attitudes are beginning to change; the marketplace will decide.

There is now a softening of earlier exuberance. There is evidence that Blackboard, WebCT and other course management tools and systems can get in the way of efforts to *learn* and *understand*. These tools are fine for students who see the big picture but they too often fail to bring useful enhancements to students seeking active, participatory engagements with complex ideas. For students, it is the difference between just seeing presentations and debating them with difficult and abstract ideas. Presentation tools have their place, but in general are limited to a small domain of the learning spectrum. Ultimately, the future of e-learning is linked to educational change and reform. The full potential of electronically-mediated instruction will not be realized unless and until large numbers of faculty members come to believe that they can use these tools for substantially improving the educational quality of their instruction, especially for undergraduates.

In the near term, there is likely to be a slowing in the adoption of e-learning. One niche area of learning where educational technology is making a big improvement is in technologies for lab courses, as mentioned before. There is something good about getting down and dirty by cleaning Petri dishes or from the clouds of smoke from uncertain experiments gone awry. But the improvements afforded by technology will more than make up for it in better learning and safety.[32]

Nor can videoconferencing be overlooked. This twenty-one-year-old medium has been vastly improved and is finally getting some respect. The California State University system, along with the University of California system, the California Community College, and the Corporation for Education Network Initiatives in California (nonprofit groups that operate the California Research and Education Network) are planning new and improved videoconferencing systems. They are creating a new network, compatible with standard Internet Protocol (IP) networks. It

---

32. "Why the E-Learning Boom Went Bust," in *The Chronicle of Higher Education*, July 9, 2004, pp. B6-B8.

will facilitate the holding of classes, meetings and collaborations on research. Scheduling will be through the existing 4CNet, a network that connects all Cal State campuses and community college campuses. Robert Mahowald, a spokesman for IDC of Framingham, Massachusetts, says that "with the emergence of very-low cost desktop cameras and technology that better navigates IP networks, people can do this stuff now. It's becoming more of a staple."[33]

Schools and colleges are now beginning to make widespread use of a new communication tool called a web log, or "blog" as it is more commonly known. A blog is a site in cyberspace that searches for and gathers together Internet articles, and plays host to virtual meetings. It can also update information on virtually any topic. It is hosted by a real person who helps to find the information required. This new communication medium is now reaching into the classroom. The technology has been around since about 1990, and was used originally by researchers at the prestigious Centre Européen pour la Recherche Nucléaire (CERN) in Switzerland. It is now very common. Howard Dean, Governor of New Hampshire and Presidential candidate in the 2004 Presidential campaign, used a blog effectively to debate and discuss issues with voters. School children are now using this technology to write reviews of books they have read. And graduate students use blogs to collaborate with colleagues in real time. It is a personal medium that easily connects people with common interests.

Even the US Army is in the e-learning business. Soldiers having at least three years of active service time are now eligible to enroll in their new e-learning program, eArmyU. Students can select from more than 2,000 courses and 90 degree programs offered through a consortium of some 20 highly regarded colleges and universities. Their books are paid for and can be sent to the individual's home address. These programs are offered at 11 military installations worldwide. Some 31,000 soldier students are enrolled, more than 5 percent of the Army's total ranks, and this program is on track to expand to additional sites. It projected 80,000 enlistees in 2005.[34]

---

33. *The Chronicle of Higher Education*, May 23, 2003, p. A30.

Overriding these various opportunities for wider and better access to higher education are copyright issues. The Technology, Education, and Copyright Harmonization Act, which became law in 2002, sets limits and standards as to how administrators operate their distance-education programs. The Act explicitly puts the obligation on the institution, not the individual instructor, to develop policy in areas of copyright interpretation, such as access and distribution in this area of copyright law.

3. BUSINESS INFORMATION & LIBRARY SYSTEMS

Once merely a means to speed up access to information and reduce management and clerical costs, IT systems have now become a key source of competitive advantage. IT is not simply just the Enterprise Resource Planning (ERP) systems which manage the institution or company in regard to funds flow, scheduling and information management. It also includes the gamut of technology systems which aid and enable improved ways of learning, including ERP. IT enables the institution to find and enroll better students; schedule classes more efficiently, make more linkages with industries and with other outside partners, and track alumni prospects over the years for institutional giving. It includes online and distance learning systems, research investigations, virtual laboratories and a host of other applications. The complexity of the technology will increase: from earlier large mainframe information engines, to knowledge and course management systems, to Web services, personal handheld and other devices used by students, faculty and staff for virtually everything. Colleges and universities are quite dependent upon IT, and they must have the wisdom to know how best to manage this technology. Having said this, the fact is that they are *not* reaping the rewards they should. Why is this?

There is a kind of love-hate relationship between the users and the administrators of the ERP systems which drive information systems. There is fierce competition among the major system providers, such as

---

34. "Online Ed: it's in the Army Now," in *The U.S. News & World Report*, October 28, 2002, p. 58.

Systems & Computer Technology Corp. (SCT), Oracle/PeopleSoft and SAP and others to implement and support them. These systems manage the financial, human resource, payroll processing and student systems needed to manage these complex enterprises.

Selecting the right vendor for a college or university is one of the most important decisions any institution will make. Once it is in, it is in to stay. That is, it is a major effort and expense to implement such systems, maintain them, and carry out the periodic upgrades and improvements needed. The costs of changing an ERP vendor can be unimaginable. The best single piece of advice today regarding system selection is to involve all parties in the selection and implementation process. It is not just the president, senior administration and IT people who should call the shots regarding system selection and features. It must also involve human resources, students, alumni, research groups, academic units and others as equal partners.

Administrators have but three things to consider in terms of computing systems: make, value, and quality of interfaces with the World Wide Web. The first involves upgrading existing systems and software using best of breed technologies along with applications developed in-house, when needed. The second is to install one of the major ERP systems. This option brings integrated power for operating efficiency, decision making and communication, and requires software consultants to do the necessary integration and training. The third concern is the need to tie into the Web for functionality, and to develop custom features for particular applications. All these options can be very costly, and all require continual updating of software.

There are five areas that every President/Chancellor and senior administrative cabinet member needs to consider properly in order to realize the potential benefits of institutional IT. [35]

1. *The President owns and is responsible for institutional IT strategy.*

The president must accept personal responsibility for the institution's IT strategy. That does not mean that he/she needs to have a tech-

---

35. "Six IT Decisions Your IT People Shouldn't Make," *Harvard Business Review*, November 2002, pp. 85-91.b

nical interest or understanding of the information technology per se. But it does mean that, because IT is a key component of the overall institutional vision, the president must personally and visibly embrace it as vital to strategy, growth, quality and competitiveness. It also means that he/she, working with senior academics and administrators, must take personal ownership of the technology program. Specifically, the president needs to set and stick to the level of IT spending needed in the strategic plan to achieve the various objectives. Instead of approaching IT decision-making in an ad hoc manner, institutions are increasingly establishing formal IT governance structures that specifically spell out just how IT decisions are made, carried out, reinforced and challenged. Good IT governance identifies who should be responsible and accountable for critical IT decisions.

2. *Senior IT administrative officials own IT processes.*

It is the responsibility of all senior IT administrators to own the institutional IT processes: choosing proper technology standards, deciding upon the design and operations of central data and business centers, and all the skills and staffing needed to support the IT mission. These professionals are to develop those processes and implementation methods that will meet long-term institutional goals and requirements. It is then is up to senior IT managers to make regular contact with the president and with other key senior academic leaders to ensure that the strategy and the goals mesh efficiently.

3. *Built-in quality for IT services.*

All users should expect quality in their administrative IT services. However, not all services need to be constantly of Six Sigma quality. A few service areas may need high levels of access and dependability, but most should operate outside a narrow, but acceptable, band of limited downtime and slow response at certain expected and stated times. Fixed costs can be made lower by determining actual requirements for response time and reliability. And too many institutions are not getting the informational value they should expect, given their considerable technology investments. It is the joint responsibility of the president's office and senior IT professionals to set appropriate service level standards.

4. System security and privacy.

Security and privacy are twin features that usually trade off with cost and user convenience. Firewalls and user access must be designed to protect system integrity. And greater security may constrain the use of certain application software packages. This is an area in which competing institutions may want frequently to share experience and develop inside and outside benchmarks.

5. Ongoing training.

The Achilles heel of most institutional IT services is the lack of convenient ways for students, faculty and administrators to be trained and to learn to use these systems. The value of any IT system investment is in direct proportion to the care taken to provide such ongoing training online and with individual and groups. Trainers need appropriate incentives to take their role seriously.

Academic computing is usually treated and managed as separate from institutional IT needs, and is handled at university, school, college or department level. This area of IT provides for student and research projects. Funding comes from department budgets and from government and private-sector-sponsored research programs and from donations. It tends to be a shadow operation in that much of the maintenance and ongoing costs are buried within departmental budgets.

Colleges and universities are becoming ever more connected with the power of open-source code projects, like Linux, Apache Web server software and uPortal, by which colleges enable the building of campus-wide Web portals. But it will take time for administrators to build their confidence in these noncommercial tools, which are often difficult to get vendors to stand behind. Moreover, free software abounds: operating systems, databases, web servers, tools and office suites.[36] Caveat emptor!

Experience to date suggests that much of the capital and time invested in IT systems for institutions of higher education has failed to produce the desired results.[37] Various studies have shown that in 30 to 75

---

36. *The Chronicle of Higher Education,* Aug. 1, 2003, pp. A31-32.
37. "When Too Much IT Knowledge is a Dangerous Thing," in the *MIT Sloan Management Review,* Winter 2003, pp. 83-89.

percent of cases, new systems do not live up to expectations, register a measurable financial impact, improve work processes, or bring about organizational change. This is a damning indictment both for industry and for institutions. The basic issue appears to be that managers considering a new system installation generally follow what amounts to a universal checklist, one that is supposed to provide for all foreseeable situations. However, experience shows that managers do not always need more IT capacity, but rather to anticipate the future uses and application of the system—and then size the ERP installation accordingly.

McAfee, the antivirus software company, has identified five pitfalls that commonly appear, despite management's best efforts: inertia, resistance, misspecification, misuse and nonuse.

Inertia: the inability to complete the installation on time. It thwarts progress during the implementation, even when all parties appear to have agreed about the particulars of the project.

Resistance: when people are not coordinated in regard to how, or even whether, the implementation should proceed. This occurs when staff incentives are threatened because of extra burdens of work which may compromise workers' base responsibilities.

Misspecification: occurs when a project has a high level of complexity, with the consequence that although meeting the technical objectives, fails to deliver the expectations set out.

Misuse: occurs when users of the new system are unsophisticated about the technology and try to get it to do things it was not intended to do. At its worst, errors can multiply, crippling the new system.

Nonuse: occurs when the new technology is in some way regarded as optional, so people default to their past ways and ignore the new opportunities.

McAfee offers several guidelines and ground rules that can be helpful in getting the installation working to everyone's expectations. They offer the following advice:

First, the implementation should be treated as a business change project, not just a technology installation. Active leadership should come from the business side, and clear responsibilities for projects and outcomes must be assigned. If no one owns a given part of the project, pitfalls will likely go unnoticed and failure will likely follow.

Then, be sure to secure specific senior institutional management commitments, and have these leaders actively involved in the project, from start to finish. This commitment should be in the form of a memo of understanding which details their specific tasks and guidance, shared among all key project members. Most implementation leaders will be eager to pitch in, but some just may not know how, when or where.

Next, the necessary resources to the project need to be identified and set aside. One of the toughest aspects of resource planning is when to assign the best people to the project, including needed outside consultants. The bills are expensive, but what is more important than making this far-reaching enterprise a real success? Cutting corners in such efforts simply makes no sense.

Also, make sure that the project's goals, scope and expectations are clear from the outset in order to get everyone involved. Many implementations have been badly oversold from the outset, in both terms of how easy the execution will be, and how quickly benefits will be seen by users. Many implementation projects become bloated and drag on as the project's scope widens, and managers struggle to keep control. Implementation leaders must ensure that user groups have a shared understanding of what is going to happen, and what is not. Any implementation can succeed in the absence of detailed cost and return calculations, but simply cannot without a set of well-articulated goals.

It is absolutely vital that the project's progress, results and scope are tracked continuously. This advice may sound trite, but many project managers have been shocked at how their organizations tend to neglect such tracking. As a result, stakeholders do not know whether or not the project is within specified parameters, has met designated milestones, and will produce the measurable performance improvements expected of the new system.

Finally, the success of the project is secured only when the new system project is tested in every way possible before it goes live. There will be some surprises just after a project goes online, but they can be limited by a thorough testing program. A word of warning: trying to run old and new systems in parallel usually does not work; it only breeds confusion about which system is the right one.

Attention will now turn to another vital source of important information for colleges: libraries. Once the cornerstone of scholarly and leisurely pursuits, libraries now struggle to survive in an era of instant, on-demand information. College and university libraries once were seen as hoarders, or protectors of information, absolutely vital. Books were to be kept on shelves, in certain catalogued places, accessible only at certain times. They were treasures.

Nowadays, of course, students and researchers look beyond the stacks of books, to the internet for much of their information. The stacks are still there, but new scholars need to be informed also about modern access to information. Libraries are no less vital to scholars than previously; only the modes of access have changed.

As an example, SUNY (the State University of New York) has a statewide contract for library software to serve and integrate all 64 of its campuses, via a shared virtual catalog of nearly 18 million records.[38] Its vendor agreement requires it to complete a copy of the software source code and all related documentation, to be held in escrow so that, just in case, it will always have access to the source code that makes the system work. About half of all periodicals and scholarly journals in SUNY libraries are on track to be accessible from anywhere, by students and faculty members who can log on to the system from any Web browser. Its library software creates a single electronic catalog and system for circulation, acquisition, and administration for the university's 70-odd libraries, while still permitting librarians to exercise their authority locally.

And now there are e-books.[39] This new technology supplies digital versions of books to libraries, much the same way publishers sell hardcopy books to them. Overall, the e-book market nationally is building steadily, to about 3 million copies in 2005. Companies involved include

---

38. *The Chronicle of Higher Education*, Dec. 8, 2000, p. A37
39. *The Wall Street Journal*, March 12, 2001, p. R34.

netLibrary Inc., Questia Media Inc., and ebary Inc. NetLibrary sells digital versions of books to academic and other libraries. Publishers like the fact that their material is tightly controlled; if a library orders only a single copy of an e-book from netLibrary, only one patron at a time can access the book. Other companies provide rental services to college students and other groups. Subscribers get what they want, but no longer have to store their books on shelves. And students can use digitized materials to write term papers in their rooms, avoiding having to trudge back and forth to the library. They can browse a book online, get hard copies of the materials they want, and authors get a piece of copy action, around the clock.

Carnegie-Mellon University (CMU) is a pioneer in the use of this modern "libratechnology." Some of its findings are given below.

- 50 percent of what a typical academic library buys will be in digital format in the year 2020.
- Digital information costs from 25 to over 300 percent more than paper information.
- Cost of converting paper to digital resources (when copyright has expired or permission has been obtained) runs from about $100 to $500 per volume.
- CMU journal expenditures have increased by almost 600 percent in the past 20 years, 4-5 times the economy's inflation rate.
- Electronic versions of existing journals sell for a fraction of paper subscription costs.
- Diversification into formats such as slides, videos, computer programs and compact disks is technically feasible as bandwidth and storage capacity increase, but will require new library strategies.
- Computer storage will not be a constraint in an environment where a petabyte (10^{15} bytes) will hold the contents of a billion books (more than have ever been published).

For more, see www.library.cmu.edu/Libraries.

4. Managing and Reining in Technology Costs

It is not a secret that direct and indirect IT costs for colleges and universities are soaring. Nor is it a secret that, among students and senior administrators, few believe that they are getting good value for their investments. Most systems and software seem to become obsolete almost as soon as they are up and running. Added to all this is the tendency for faculties to expect to use their own pet packages rather than be team members and agree to consensus choices. This has the effect of proliferating problems and costs, and can be a real burden to students.

A case in point is a research study conducted by the author in 2001 that focused on leading undergraduate engineering programs. It was found that fully half of these programs used multiple Course Management Systems (CMS). These are large, complex and costly packages which run on a school's ERP system and to which faculty can make assignments, for example. CMS allows virtual collaboration to be quite convenient. And the trend seems to be toward even more proliferation, so that package, maintenance and training costs will continue to rise. It is an emotive issue everywhere. Adherents of a particular CMS system see those with different preferences as simpleminded. The issue tends to split students, faculty and administrators alike. Never mind that students have been well educated for a millennium without such technology. And there is no solid evidence to date that CMS systems actually lead students to a more durable understanding of the material being studied.

IT costs can easily rise and strangle an institution with excessive one-off and recurring costs. No elixir is better than having appropriate standards for use:
- Train all who will use the system
- Inform users how to use the systems appropriately, and make sure they know that access isn't free
- Control and prioritize access.

The certainty is that escalating costs associated with communications, software, help-desks and related administrative salaries and services will continue until institutional leaders make tough, often unpopular, decisions. Dr. Martin Ringle, Director of Computing & Information Services, at Reed College, Portland,[40] proffers eight ways in which colleges and universities can cut spiraling IT costs:

---

40. "10 Ways Colleges Can Cut IT Costs," in The *Chronicle of Higher Education*, October 4, 2002, pp. A39-43.

1) Cap the bandwidth and end dial-up modem service in dormitories.

Bandwidth is the amount of information per second that can be carried through a physical communication linkup: phone line, copper or optical fiber, or satellite feed. (A standard telephone transmits 54,000 bits per second. A T1 circuit can move 1.54 million bits a second, nearly 30 times as fast.) Most modern communication infrastructures are fiber-optic, although there are some remaining copper, which is much slower. It is expensive and the thirst for it seems endless. Transmission of text information is relatively inexpensive, but can get quite costly when using movie downloads, DVDs and such. It taxes network capacity and requires more and more costly system components to accommodate the demand. Certainly, much of dormitory-use bandwidth is consumed in legitimate academic pursuits, but much is for recreational entertainment, which chews up bandwidth and costs, day and night. Dial-up modem services, such as AOL, are slow, but they are free and have become a kind of student entitlement. As with other services, colleges and universities may consider not providing free access for students working (and playing) in dorms or off-campus apartments, just as students are expected to pay for their personal telephone calls. To combat this source of cost, many institutions are placing various kinds of caps on dorm bandwidth, and partnering with outside providers for lower bandwidth rates.

2) Do not invest in phone systems that students will not use.

It once seemed, for many schools, to be a good idea: the college would install and maintain a private branch exchange (PBX), which would then provide a long-distance phone service for everyone in the institution. After all, PBX systems can be much less costly than using conventional phone providers. However, the rapid growth of cell phone use, now by a majority of students, is making the PBX service seem medieval and unattractive. And the intended revenue from students calling long distance is evaporating. Looking ahead, a new technology—Internet Protocol Telephony—may be an even better option.

3) Collaborate with other colleges to sign joint licenses for software.

Software costs for administrative and research functions will continue to soar. Much of it is for proprietary licenses for course management systems, such as Blackboard, WebCT and others. Some institutions are standardizing on one or two systems in order to lessen the costs of multiple platforms. Others are beginning to look at partnerships with other, closely located institutions to share a single license, thereby cutting each institution's costs in half. Another strategy is to migrate gradually away from proprietary software such as Microsoft Windows and MS Office, and toward open-source software such as Linux, StarOffice and Open Office. These platforms generally do not charge software license fees, and they allow wider latitude for students and research teams. This approach can enable schools and colleges to develop the customized course management systems discussed above.

4) Use students to handle help-desk questions at night.

Computer help-desks provide a vital service to both students and teaching staff. Larger institutions generally offer round-the-clock support, but the demand is not uniform. So, rather than use staffing consultants during off-peak hours, some institutions are employing student hot line computer services during those times. Student computer whizzes can solve many problems over the phone, and record more difficult ones for professional staff or consultants to deal with.

5) Create limits or rules for students' printouts.

Free printouts by students are often taken to excess, and much of it is wasted/trashed. It also costs materially in printer maintenance and other administrative support. One way to deal with this growing problem is to limit printers to just a very few stations in order to make the service just a little inconvenient. Some other institutions charge a small fee for printer services, mainly so that users will be more aware that printing costs someone.

6) Join purchasing pools for hardware and other IT expenses.

Pooling purchases of IT equipment can save a lot of money. This is easiest within state institutions that have multiple campuses, but it works nearly as well among cooperative purchasing groups of nonaffiliated, nearby colleges and universities. Such pools can also consolidate administration and technology operations, saving even more money.

7) Use life cycle planning to centralize desktop purchases.

Institutions have many approaches to the purchasing, maintenance and retirement of desktop computers, handheld computer appliances and related application software. Some schools buy or lease such equipment and services; others require students to purchase their own from an approved list. A shrinking number have no policy whatsoever. Buying desktop systems without constraint or with little policy only leads to more costly software and servicing. A growing number of schools are looking at machine and software costs as commodities, with finite lives. They are buying in large bulk, and are replacing their equipment after a short period (usually three years), which ensures that all such equipment is no older that that. And they enter into maintenance agreements with their vendors to keep their equipment up and running all the time.

8) Use a single preferred provider for technology purchases.

Purchasing administrators can cut costs by changing from their customary policy of buying IT equipment and services via a number of preferred providers, and moving toward long-term contracts with a single vendor. The vendor can then create a Web site which enables students and others to buy the desktops, notebooks and other computer-related products they need, and often at a fraction of the cost. And the preferred provider may also enter into a technical support agreement with the institution.

5. INSTITUTIONAL IT POLICY

The first step toward reining in IT costs is to equip the institution, the faculty, teaching assistants and all appropriate others with the knowledge needed regarding learning processes which are central to education. Administrators must have the appropriate training in technology and related policy. Examples extend to technologies dealing with collaborative administrative processes, inquiry and project-based learning, technology-enhanced teaching and learning, instructional design, cross-discipline teaching, teaching assessment and educational outcomes. This investment in training and awareness will pay off handsomely.

Secondly, there are some key policy areas that must be articulated and shared widely with all concerned: class sizes and configurations; office hours, attendance requirements, intellectual property, honor codes; privacy and personal space (a huge issue in the new learning environment); and issues related to faculty status, facilities, equipment and technical support; helpdesks; and platforms for content development and presentation. Moreover, policies are needed in the area of faculty support for creating online and other presentation materials. As technology's impact on pedagogy becomes more pervasive, every college and university will need to develop a comprehensive institutional strategy designed for its own particular use.

There must also be a policy on privacy regarding the use of technology and information. All institutions should now have policies governing privacy, including such issues as when administrators may examine a student's e-mail and other electronic files, spying and electronic theft. The following are policies taken from five distinguished institutions:

University of California System: "The University does not routinely inspect, monitor, or disclose electronic communications without the holder's consent. When under the circumstances described above the contents of electronic communications must be inspected, monitored, or disclosed without the holder's consent...such actions must be authorized in advance and in writing by the responsible campus vice chancellor or, for the office of the president, the senior vice president, business & finance."

Cornell University: "The University reserves the right to limit access to its networks when applicable university policies or codes, contractual obligations, or state or Federal laws are violated, but it does not monitor or generally restrict the content of material transported across those networks."

The University of Pennsylvania: "While the University does not generally monitor or access the contents of a student's e-mail or computer accounts, it reserves the right to do so. However, access to and disclosure of a student's e-mail messages and the contents of his or her computer accounts may only be authorized by any of the deans of the student's school, or his/her designate, the vice provost for university life, or the office of audit and compliance, in consultation with the office of the general counsel."

University of Tennessee at Knoxville: "The University does not routinely examine the content of a user's account space; however, it reserves the right to investigate the use of that account and to inspect the account contents when deemed necessary."

Wayne State University: "While respecting user's privacy to the fullest extent possible, the University reserves the right to examine any computer files...No action under this section may be taken by university officers without the approval of the president or his/her designee."

Clearly, administrative computing systems are vital to any educational institution. They are also very expensive to maintain, and need continuing maintenance and upgrading just to keep up with needs of faculty, students, researchers and administrators. As John Curry, Executive Vice President of MIT, said, "Some of us have seen fortunes slip through our hands as we learned how to implement these kinds of systems in universities."

Setting technology policy in an academic environment can be tricky, but it is absolutely essential. Each member of the institution can have a voice in just about every issue. Therefore, policy evolves slowly and with a great deal of deliberation. Dr. Martin Ringle, of Reed College in Portland, Oregon,[41] offers a list of ten critical issues for technology planning. The following are excerpts:

- Establish a rigorous, cohesive and disciplined process for the planning and budgeting of integrated IT and related information resources, including instructional computing, research computing, administrative computing, library resources, media services and telecommunications. The process should touch all these organizational sectors; should define roles and responsibilities; and should be honed and refined periodically.

---

41. Internet article by Dr. Martin Ringle of Reed College, Portland, OR, ringlet@reed.edu.

- Establish an institution-wide policy for allocating, upgrading, repairing and replacing computer equipment that will ease the financial burden on all in the long run. Aging equipment can be a barrier to accessing electronic resources. The ideal is for budgets to be established sufficiently to replace computer equipment every five years.
- Evaluate technology investments based upon how well they will serve the institutional mission. Find even better ways of assessing and measuring the effectiveness of these investments, before and during their use.
- Continually explore consortia or collaborative relationships with nearby technology vendors, maintenance services and with other academic institutions to provide technology and information resources in the most cost-effective ways that will serve students and faculty even better.
- Provide for easy electronic communication beyond the campus, with alumni, parents, prospective students, scholars at other institutions and prospective employers. Campus networks and portals can be valuable sources for knitting these communities together for mutual benefit and collaborations.
- Establish a campus-wide policy that covers the important ethical and legal guidelines for the use of facilities, including the Internet, electronic mail and the WWW. All institutions, but especially small, budget-challenged colleges, can gain enormous benefits from educational technologies. Make sure policy issues such as fair use, censorship, etc., are covered.
- Establish a policy which covers ownership and/or royalties for electronic materials produced by faculty or other members of the college community. This policy should provide for faculty and staff to sign formal agreements of ownership regarding new technology tools and content.
- Issue institutional policy and guidelines for faculty, library staff, technology and college counsel that apply to copyright, licensing and library materials and rights, conventional and electronic access and issues. These issues are getting ever more complex and need ongoing attention.
- Provide ample opportunities for faculty to use the power of the www, the multimedia and other new instructional technologies which can enhance the learning experience to its full potential for teaching, student recruitment, campus information, public relations and other purposes. Arrange for ongoing tutorials for faculty and staff so they can become knowledgeable and comfortable with educational technologies. Again, all institutions—but especially smaller ones with modest endowments—can gain much from the Web. But make sure practical and policy issues such as censorship, fair use, etc., are addressed and heeded.

Colleges and universities are getting ever larger, more complex, and entangled in litigious matters. Institutions are more prone than ever to missteps that can upset orderly policies and processes. Some of the policy needs which require much more attention are listed below.

01. Honor code (including plagiarism and other forms of cheating)
02. Facilities, technologies, equipment and technical support
03. Class sizes and configurations
04. Office hours (real, virtual)
05. Attendance requirements
06. Helpdesks
07. Privacy and personal space
08. Use of and access to intellectual property
09. Platforms for content development and presentations
10. Faculty member status
11. Advisory and visiting boards

6. Benchmarking

Benchmarking is an invaluable measurement tool used for improving business processes. A benchmark is simply a quantitative measure of a relevant business element which provides useful knowledge for future improvement. It may measure speed, defects, on-time delivery, flexibility, customer satisfaction, and a host of other similar features. Collectively, a set of benchmarks can be used for continuous improvement for any kind of enterprise, including academic institutions. Benchmarking is enormously important because it forces the institution to set meaningful targets, and to improve upon and measure those targets, year on year. These two facets have been absolutely crucial to the industrial sector becoming ever more efficient, to the benefit of enterprises of all kinds. This philosophy is finding its way into educational institutions.

Experience has shown that benchmarks can be grouped within six broad categories:

- Speed
- Quality (defects/errors)
- Waste

- Financial
- Updating skills
- Customer satisfaction

Many industrial companies use upwards of a hundred or more specific metrics within these six categories, measured annually, quarterly or on a per shift basis as needed, to create a living report card of how well they are doing against planned targets. Any organization can take these six categories and assign one or several specific targets within each to aim for. These targets may range from the general, such as "customer satisfaction," to quite specific measures such as "errors per million opportunities to make an error."

As discussed in Chapter III.5, many industrial companies have embraced some approach to an overall quality platform, such as the well-known Six Sigma methodology protocol developed by Motorola for the continuing elimination of errors, and time, and other, wastage. Within these categories they can then develop meaningful, specific, quantitative measures for process improvements.

It is, of course, much easier for industry to measure errors in these six categories than it is for an educational enterprise. But that cannot be an excuse for not doing it. Measurements must be crafted within institutions of higher educations, at least to a level that it provides guidance for betterment.

In educational institutions, there must be a clear and specific quantitative method of measuring each of the six categories. And there must also be a standard which identifies who makes these measurements accurately, when, and how. Examples of elements within each category are given below.

- Speed: Financial transactions; student time-to-degree cycles
- Quality: College ratings; retention of best faculty and staff; application/admission ratio
- Waste: Better utilization of classrooms and other facilities around the calendar; lost physical materials
- Financial: Endowment returns; reduced costs; leasing vs. purchases
- Continual skills updating: Programs to enable administrators and staff; and for faculty and teaching assistants.

- Customer satisfaction: Growth of new admissions; reduction in student transfers

The experience of those companies who have embraced the discipline of benchmarking is that they have profited quite significantly from improved operational efficiency and customer loyalty. And the same benefits await those leading educators looking for better ways to improve their operations and services.

7. LIBRARIES

As with everything else, the IT age is affecting institutional libraries quite fundamentally. How will they be managed and staffed in the future? Despite the trend to use online information sources, there are increasing pressures for more shelf space for collections, and for more students to be trained in librarianship. Students working together on team projects still need libraries, and they demand speed of access.

Major academic libraries have about 40 percent of their journals available in full text, but they go back only a few years. Increasing storage and space restrictions no longer allow the stockpiling of journals as before. As one measure, Pennsylvania State University has some two million books in its engineering stacks and another 10-15 thousand full-text books online. Incremental costs are soaring. The traditional rule of thumb has been to double library space every five years. That time frame is getting much smaller.

New serials and journals are multiplying, and acquisition costs for such sources as Compendix, Engineering Index, and others, are rising at around 6 percent each year, despite flat budgets; costs just continue to rise. Academic libraries are being forced to cancel some of their subscriptions each year. And the role of the librarian is also changing accordingly, from one of helper and order taker, to that of a coach training students to become more self-sufficient in their information needs. Because students are working more than ever with their colleagues and in chat rooms, more training is needed for them to access their information needs.

Many schools are migrating from their in-house library systems to turnkey vendor solutions. For example, RPI (Rensselaer Polytechnic Institute) is outsourcing its in-house library system to Innovative Interfaces, Inc. A web OPAC (online public assess catalog) interface now replaces its former command-driven Infotrax system, resulting in better efficiencies, greater user satisfaction and better tracking and utilization of resources. Many others are doing likewise. The trend for the great universities is to turn away from recreating holdings; instead, putting their resources into creating dynamic, virtual libraries that can provide near 100 percent access and minimal print needs.

Chapter V: The New Business of Higher Education

The New Business of Higher Education

Topical Themes
1. Core Academic Values: Leadership, Academic Policy, Ethics, Branding
2. Universities Emulating Businesses
3. The Cost Structure and Economics of Higher Education
4. Tenure and Collective Bargaining

1. Core Academic Values: Leadership, Academic Policy, Ethics, Branding

The operations and processes of higher education institutions will continue to get more complex, as complex as the large industrial giants, because of the widening range of missions they must serve. Colleges and universities are called to teach scholarship and learning, develop character among its members, conduct basic and applied research that benefits society, and to provide public and private community services, ranging from athletics to health care. This chapter probes the need and nature for this wide-ranging set of obligations. It will address some of the more important components of the modern college and university from various viewpoints, but with a focus on core academic values, institutional leadership and branding, business roles, cost structure and economics, university presses, and the international role of institutions, including tenure and collective bargaining among various faculty members. Because of these many and disparate obligations, higher learning institutions are often more complex to administer than others in the public and private sectors. Indeed, this is precisely the reason that academia has tried to master a wide collection of leadership roles, including distributed leadership. Some succeed; most do not.

Leadership

A good way for an institution to assess the extent of improvements needed is for it to consider its current place on what may be called the "staircase to success." This has three steps, ranging from struggling to exemplary, and the characteristics of each step are suggested by a group of descriptors. Institutions may not fit precisely onto any one of these steps, but they will find it revealing to identify those elements among the three steps that presently apply to them.

STEP 1. Widespread Improvements Needed
- tradition-bound
- bureaucratic; experimenting with quality & flexibility
- safe
- incremental improvements
- procedural
- struggling with uneven quality
- avoids taking risks
- occasional process improvements
- survivor by being a follower
- moderate student satisfaction

STEP 2. Scattered Areas of Excellence
- moderate risk-takers
- solid quality
- determined
- effective leadership
- stress on building teamwork & cooperation
- focused processes
- continuing education
- embraces flexibility

- striving & aspiring for betterment
- improving processes
- finding and implementing a vision
- active areas of continuing improvement
- branding awareness
- pleased students

STEP 3. Icon of Excellence
- leader, risk-taker and innovator
- a living, strategic intent instrument
- teamwork & flexibility as the norm
- life-long learning
- focus on efficiencies
- developing & inspiring minds
- icons of quality
- market-focused
- highly-effective leadership
- being the best it can
- meeting & besting their institutional vision
- delighted students
- optimized processes
- highly efficient use of buildings, faculty & services

Being the president or chancellor of a college or university is one of the toughest jobs imaginable. The academic head of ship has easily as challenging a role as that of any large corporate head. Presidents function as the chief executive officer of the institution. They have multiple responsibilities, the main ones being to create and embed an institutional vision; lead and negotiate with loyal and fractious groups of faculty, staff and students; and to support the loyalties of alumni, politicians and donors. Moreover, presidents often lack some of the authority which industrial leaders enjoy, owing to long-honored traditions that give faculty members considerable latitude and independence. They are also accountable to a board of trustees or governors, which functions as the equivalent of the board of directors in the corporate/private sector. They oversee other advisory committees and councils that work with them. And as a president is also a member of the faculty, this person is more vulnerable to the slings and arrows of this most powerful group. The presidency is a very demanding and stressful office.

The various duties of a university president were captured with great candor in an address by the esteemed Clark Kerr, then Chancellor of the University of California system, on the occasion of the Godkin lectures he delivered at Harvard. The following excerpts show that his insights are as relevant today as when he made these remarks in 1963.

> It is sometimes said that the American multiversity president is a two-faced character. This is not so. If he were, he could not survive. He is a many-faced character, in the sense that he must face in many directions at once while contriving not to turn his back on any important group.
>
> The American university president is expected to be a friend of the students; a colleague of the faculty; a good fellow with the alumni; a sound administrator with the trustees; a good speaker with the public; an astute bargainer with the foundations and the Federal agencies; a politician with the state legislature; a friend of industry; labor and agriculture; a persuasive diplomat with donors; a champion of education generally; a supporter of the professions—particularly law and medicine; a spokesman to the press; a scholar in his own right; a public servant at the state and national levels; a devotee of opera and football equally; a decent human being; a good husband and father and an active member of a church. Moreover, he must be seen as enjoying traveling in airplanes, eating his meals in public and attending public ceremonies. No one can be all of these things. Some succeed at being none.
>
> He should be firm, yet gentle; sensitive to others but insensitive to himself; look to the past and the future, yet be firmly planted in the present; he should be both visionary and sound, affable yet reflective; know the value of a dollar and realize that ideas cannot be bought; inspiring in his visions yet cautious in what he does; a man of principle yet able to make a deal; a man with broad perspective who will follow the details conscientiously; a good American but ready to criticize the status quo fearlessly; a seeker of truth where the truth may not hurt too much; a source of public-policy pronouncements when they do not reflect on his own institution. He is one of the marginal men in a democratic society—of whom there are many others—working on the margin of many groups, many ideas, many endeavors, and many characteristics.
>
> The President of the modern multiversity is leader, educator, creator, initiator and wielder of power and pump. He is also officeholder, caretaker, inheritor, consensus-seeker, persuader and bottleneck. But his is *mostly* as a mediator. To make the multiversity work really effectively, the moderates need to be in control of each power center. And there needs to be an attitude of tolerance between and among the power centers, with few territorial ambitions. When the extremists get in control of the students, the faculty, or the trustees with class-warfare concepts, then the "delicate balance of interests" becomes an actual war. Instead of *power* being commensurate with responsibility, the *opportunity to persuade*, for the president, should be commensurate with the responsibility. He must have ready access to each center power, a fair chance in each forum of opinion, a chance to paint reality in place of illusion and to argue the cause of reason.

Because of the stresses and expectations placed on this position, colleges are increasingly looking outside of academe for new presidents. In 1998, some 6 percent of college presidents came from outside higher education; by 2001 it had risen to 12 percent, and continues to rise. Theodore J. Marchese, Managing Director of Academic Search Consultation Service, a search firm in Washington, D.C., says "From a board member's standpoint, if you define the president's job in terms of the things you see your president talking about at board meetings—fund raising, politics, marketing, financial management, and still more fund raising—more than a few candidates from outside the academy seem to present competitive portfolios." Some of the things Boards of Trustees look for include well-honed political skills, business savvy, leadership and a good feel of handling related outside affairs.[42]

The president's job today has expanded to include a much wider scope than from the duties of just two decades ago. Indeed, the modern president is hard pressed to do it alone. Provosts are routinely seen to be running what is analogous to the office of Chief Operating Officer in the corporate sector. They still manage curriculum, faculty development, tenure and academic affairs, but in the past few years they have increasingly taken on roles that used to belong to the president exclusively. Boards of trustees insist on it.

Donna Shalala, formerly both President of the University of Miami and the US Secretary of Health and Human Services, has seen this shift. She says that presidents now are taking on more development, capital, and other fund-raising initiatives, while tasking the provost to take on more of the operational agenda: planning and budgeting, internal institutional boards and councils, athletic programs—all with a focus directed toward broad academic and civic affairs. The burdens for both are weighty, and some administrations have taken to creating teams of two, with the president and provost essentially sharing the load. For example, at the University of Arizona, President Peter Likins and Provost George Davis have worked as an indivisible team to get the work done better and faster.

---

42. "Casting a Wider Net," in The Chronicle of Higher Education, Dec. 13, 2002, p. A32-33.

According to the American Council of Education, college presidents serve, on average, about 6.6 years in that position. This period of tenure can therefore be used to evaluate just how much has been done within a particular president's span of authority. Has the officeholder been a caretaker, revolutionist or visionary? Every incumbent, each link of the chain, can be seen as a part of the unfolding history of the institution. Thoughtful academic leaders can look at past developments and then plan accordingly as to what the institution's next chapter must be.

If college presidents do much or all of the work that their corporate counterpart CEOs do, they should (and sometimes do) get roughly comparable compensation packages. The difference is that academic leaders by and large do not enjoy bonuses or stock options (the exception, of course, is in the academic for-profit sector, which does allow those perks). Moreover, today some 75 percent of presidents of public research universities are given on-campus housing and caretakers as part of their compensation packages. Also, high-profile presidents are actively sought after to serve on industrial and other boards which allows them to supplement their compensation and to interact with other peer leaders from industry and government. In addition to these conveniences, they are provided with an effective and intimate venue for discussing fund-raising initiatives with prospective donors.

Academic Policy

The president's number one responsibility is to lead, rather than command, a team that can set in motion those actions that will forge the institution's special character in the years to come. A powerful tool in forging the future of the institution is the Vision/Mission (V/M) policy statement. This is a briefly-stated set of principles which articulates the institution's values and future directions, and makes clear what the institution wants to become. The Vision portion describes the institutional roles and character in the years ahead. The Mission articulates the institutional goals which, taken together, provides a platform to support the Vision's success. What follows is a prescription that, if faithfully observed, can work for all stakeholders.[43]

Chapter V: The New Business of Higher Education

1. Devote the time needed to articulate specifically and succinctly your institution's vision: what you want to become, why, when and how. It can be incremental, or a radical departure from your current game plan. For inspiration, look at vision statements from other institutions and corporations that you admire, but grapple with the future essence and uniqueness of what your institution is to be in the years/decades ahead. In developing your Vision, be as specific as possible as to how it is to unfold—with a beginning, middle and maturity. Incorporate into your Vision a list of about five to ten carefully chosen quality metrics which, taken in combination, will help propel you toward your vision.

2. Create a Mission Statement in specific terms—one that speaks to the particular roles and needs of your institution. Why and for whom is your school needed? What are your distinguishing features? What is your approach to branding your institution? Who are your closest alliance partners and how are they to support your Vision? It falls to the President to draft this statement, then to share it with senior faculty and administrators for honing and, finally, to secure trustee approval. Many organizations provide each institutional employee with a wallet-sized card, or other device that summarizes the Vision and the Mission. These statements ought to be widely shared and referred to. It is a reflection of your institutional culture.

3. Make strategy an everyday, dynamic process that is embraced by all. The V/M statement should be referred to frequently, to keep its message fresh and alive among all the institution's stakeholders.

4. Continually challenge your institution's most valued premises, traditions and icons. This will help continually to hone your V/M over time, and will implant them in the minds of all.

5. Define your key audiences (students, faculty, donors, administrators, suppliers and friends) and develop/hone appropriate communication channels to each. Elicit, welcome and respond to feedback from these audiences.

---

43. Principles Developed at Group Schneider/Square D Company, and by Yamashita Partners, San Francisco.

6. Make decisions when and if needed; right or wrong. Waffling can erode confidence, deliver mixed messages and corrupt team-building efforts.

7. Identify those forces which might undermine your V/M. Understand and befriend them; convince and show them the benefits, and convert them. By doing this it will strengthen your V/M and your resolve to succeed.

8. Never hold a meeting that lasts longer than two hours (otherwise it is a workshop, which requires more planning). And never end a meeting without assigning a name to every item that needs follow-up. Expect—insist upon—thoughtful and timely feedback.

9. Actively invite fresh ideas from all key audiences, and do not kill any of them. Rather, keep them, for sooner or later you may need them.

10. From time to time you will find yourself at odds with key people whom you need on your side. When this happens, consider engaging a respected, independent, outside consultant who can work with faculty and administrators as a bridge to certain particular issues. This can restore the team harmony.

The issue of institutional leadership will be examined again later in this chapter.

The practice of leadership is increasingly becoming a key to the success of all educational institutions. It can be profitable in many ways by uncovering buried organizational inefficiencies. Early in the formation of America's industrial era, organizational pioneers such as Frederick Taylor and Max Weber developed ways to improve industrial productivity. They adhered to a few simple principles—among them unity of command, exception principle, and span of control. The first said that every employee is to take direction only from one supervisor. Next, the exception principle said that routine decisions should be made by employees, and that only the more far-reaching decisions were to be made by supervisors and those higher up. Finally, the span of control principle stated that there is a finite limit to the number of employees that a single supervisor can effectively manage (a few at higher levels; many more in the lower ranks). These principles had enormous influence in the nation's early history in building industrial might; they are still applicable.

But people are more sophisticated today. One of the key concepts discovered in the mid-fifties was the principle of organizational optimization. This profound principle of modern systems theory states that the only way to achieve optimal organizational efficiencies is to tackle the work of the entire organization as a single, integrated whole. If the organization is broken down into its constituent pieces instead, optimizing each of the parts in isolation from the others, and then pulling them together again will *always* result in poorer performance. This principle has proven itself in the field of systems engineering. It has profound implications for complex organizations of all kinds, including organizational behaviors in colleges and universities. Managers must focus on the entire organizational dynamics, freely exchanging plans and ideas for the betterment of the whole, not just the parts.

It takes time and persistent effort to build any effective team. Many service and industrial organizations have achieved this, by keeping a focus on measurable quality, and by continuous training of all employees. They are the cornerstones of future success. By extension, with all the rapid changes taking place in higher education, it is quite clear that new models of institutional leadership will inevitably develop to recast the way the institutions' functions will be managed.

More and more well-respected universities are competing for top status. This begs the question: To differentiate one school from another, how is excellence to be measured? The means is to establish and track appropriate metrics; otherwise it is just one opinion against another.

One particular framework[44] ranks research universities by nine specific and objective criteria:
- Total R&D expenditures
- Federally-sponsored R&D expenditures
- Number (or percentage) of members of the various National Academies
- Faculty awards
- Doctorates awarded

---

44. American Research Universities, an Annual Report developed by the University of Florida.

- Post-doctorate appointments
- SAT scores
- Endowment
- Annual Giving

These kinds of metrics should be even more finely divided in order to reveal the deeper levels of detail. For example, research expenditures can be examined by Federal and private sources, size and terms of grants and contracts, particular areas of research, and other means. The overall portfolio can then be managed, by giving more attention to research areas that the institution favors, rather than merely taking what comes along. Just as with corporations, the research mission in academia should have certain *measurable* target areas in order to meet appropriate strategic goals. Similarly, the other categories above should be further dissected in order to arrive at specific research goals.

As with any objective scale, there can be disagreement about the utility of specific scoring metrics. Nevertheless, they should include the essential factors that people see as relevant measures of excellence. Comparative evaluations should be based on the individual elements, not just a single overall score.

Colleges and universities generally do a good job in offering programs which students, and the country, need. In the years ahead, there will be both wider diversity in programs, and increasing competition among them in order to attract the best students and faculty. In the past, colleges and universities were more passive in attracting these two groups. The stakes are much higher now.

Ethics: Cheating and Honor Codes

Another difficult challenge facing all those in academe is the rising scourge of cheating, which is staining the character of higher education. This issue has been seen throughout history but there is a new and innocuous name for the practice: "scientific misconduct". One motivation arises from the intense pressure to publish the right research data and conclusions there from. The full extent of scientific misconduct cannot be fully known. Federal studies of government research have confirmed only 200 cases of blatant fraud over the past 20 years—which equates to about one person in 100,000 active researchers, per year. But others suggest that it is much more widespread, and that a blind eye is simply turned to scientific misconduct. The US Department of Health and Human Services has proposed new policies requiring institutions to educate researchers and graduate students about rules governing scientific fraud and other issues of research ethics. More of this is needed from within colleges and universities. At the core of the issue is that such conduct is wrong, and must be dealt with appropriately.

Cheating is clearly on the rise across America's campuses[45], even among the great military academies. Studies show, however, that students at schools having strict ethic codes are much less likely to cheat. So then, why do more institutions not follow suit? Why do schools not have courses and seminars on ethics? Might this help to eradicate this scourge? Part of the problem is that faculties and administrators simply have neither the time nor the inclination to take it on. They certainly do not like it, but do not know what to do about it. And they do not feel that it represents a clear and present danger to academe.

Fewer than 100 American colleges and universities have formal honor codes. The University of Virginia has the oldest. It "forbids lying, cheating, and stealing, and the only punishment is permanent expulsion." There is no formal guarantee of due process among schools that have such codes; infractions are dealt with quickly and with finality. Fraud is increasingly found in the copying of term papers from the internet and other acts of theft. And where is the line drawn between collaborating and just plain copying of course materials? As with other institutional policies, any ethics policy will be imperfect when applied to specific instances.

It seems that integrity is waning as a quality. It is not that students have lost their moral compass, but the enormous amount of information that is freely available at the touch of a button is a temptation that many find hard to resist. Colleges see it in phony term papers, dissertations and laboratory data from students at all levels. Faculty members find it hard, if not impossible, to stem this scourge.

---

45. "Honor for Honor's Sake?" in *The Chronicle of Higher Education*, May 3, 2003, pp. A35-38.

Branding

This is a market approach to attracting the best students and programs to a college or university, thereby enriching the institution. It is all about finding and broadcasting the messages that will help attract and keep the best students and faculty possible. Institutional image is, literally, big business, and colleges and universities are taking their lead from Wall Street and the mass media, and increasingly applying these tools for institutional branding purposes.

Branding uses logos and slogans to implant key messages in the minds of those that see or hear them. The benefits of branding are obvious and can be long-lasting. Some of the more prestigious institutions have gone to great lengths to legally protect their branding images. They have undertaken formal branding campaigns in order to differentiate themselves from the pack, and to raise their visibility. Among them are the Ohio State University ("Do Something Great"); the University of Florida ("Ideas that Move"); Rensselaer Polytechnic Institute ("Why Not Change the World?"); and the University of Houston ("Learning, Leading."). And what figure can be placed on the market value of Yale's *Wiff N' Poof Song*? Although not a slogan as such, this song is evocative of their alma mater and has huge branding value. Some institutions are even creating layers of intellectual protection from brand infringement.

A good illustration of brand development can be found in the University of Maryland, which, in 1997, devised five specific targets of opportunity that would launch their initiative to project a stronger image:[46]

- Identify a strong leader (preferably the president, the provost, a key vice president, or a dean) who will be the institutional champion of marketing; someone who will support and defend the strategy and results.
- Take risks—within reason. Creativity *can* stand out in a crowded field. Originality will serve you well as long as you remain true to your core values.
- Do not underestimate the desire of students to have a voice in how marketing efforts represent the institution. If you do not include them, they will be vocal in their criticism.

---

46. "Romancing the Brand," *The Chronicle of Higher Education*, Oct. 24, 2003, pp. A30-32.

- Have a thick skin. What you do is visible to everyone with your institutional affiliation. Learn to accept critical feedback graciously.
- Create branding tools appropriate to the job: a clever logo, ditty, satirical phrase, visual image, or other catchy rendering.

A logo (only *one* logo) should integrate with and support the institution's overall mission, character and vision. Many schools find that branding brings enormous tangible and intangible benefits to their institutions. The best single piece of advice is to begin by preparing the campaign carefully and with a simple, constant theme. The branding should evoke fond memories for graduates, pride among faculty and staff, and fun within the current student body and the community. If this is done properly and consistently, branding is one of the best tools an institution has for engendering goodwill and alumni giving. The branding approach works. Schools like the University of Maryland have seen substantial increases in freshmen numbers, much of it attributed to branding campaigns.

Here is yet another trend. There is a new phenomenon, the "blurring" of degrees. Faced with significant market opportunities in continuing education, an explosion of *combined* degrees, such as BA/BS, MA/MBA, and PhD/EdD is being witnessed. The University of Wisconsin at Madison has an alternate program for engineers, which integrates MBA content with various technologies. There clearly is a need for engineers and applied scientists to know more about leadership, markets, entrepreneurialism, financial practices and other topics tailored to corporate America.

Here is a checklist for presidents and chancellors, senior administrators and their trustees to consider and act upon:

Vision and Mission
- Establish the Institution's vision and mission.
- Promote institutional and personal integrity of purpose.
- Listen to and regard closely the customer, the student.
- Make a commitment to superior teaching and academic content.
- Harness appropriate uses of educational technology.
- Show respect for all within the academic community.

- Commit to fiscal integrity and leadership.
- Expect continuing improvement in all we do.

Academic Programs
- Define just what lifelong education means to the institution, and how best to implement it.
- Afford students creative ways to study abroad, both physically and virtually.

Regional Alliances
- Create meaningful coalitions with other institutions to share high cost elements such as computing,
  - Build library holdings, and other real and virtual facilities.

Finance
- Insist upon institutional teamwork across the administration, to create a culture of constructive cooperation.
- Treat fundraising as a cooperative process, involving all within the community.
- Use outsourcing as an effective way to cut costs.
- Use assets ever more efficiently.
- Gravitate toward a 12-month academic calendar, and make use of physical and intellectual assets more effectively by having students attend class at odd hours and on weekends.

Role of Technology
- Keep up with appropriate information technologies—especially as it applies to better, more effective modes of learning.
- Entertain the creation of virtual campus sites, when appropriate.

Imaging & Branding
- Create, maintain and continually improve image and branding.

Markets and Student "Pipeline"
- Create continuing alliances with 9th- to 12th-graders in the region; engage them, especially minorities, to give them a head start.
- Look carefully at underserved market segments, and cultivate them.

Faculty Issues

• Great teaching is our number one goal; this must ever be acknowledged, fostered, praised and rewarded.

• Always seek appropriate alternatives to tenure by rewarding excellence in teaching, research and providing student guidance.

• Recognize that some faculties excel in teaching, others in research and service. Acknowledge those few that do both, and seek creative ways to get the best out of both groups.

Institutional Discipline

• Put in place appropriate policies covering theft, cheating and deceit, and use these policies whenever appropriate.

Athletics

• Acknowledge that both mental and physical activity is needed for all, and therefore provide for and support appropriate athletic activity for the entire student body, faculty and staff. Collegiate athletes are expected to pursue academic excellence as their primary goal, as do all other students.

Generally, people who have chosen careers in academia were shaped in that direction quite early in life. A Pew Higher Education Research Program has shown that faculty values have been molded by the following forces: intellectual challenge (84 percent), intellectual freedom (79 percent), freedom to pursue scholarly/teaching interests (75 percent), opportunities for teaching (72 percent), autonomy (70 percent) and flexible schedule (65 percent), and research opportunities (39 percent). Many in the academic field feel an obligation to be mentors to others who are interested in the field.

2. Universities Emulating Business

Lest anyone thinks that running a university does not take business know-how, there follows a case study of how a major university can fail because of its inability to exercise leadership and manage like a business. In 1993, the Reverend John J. Piderit, SJ, was named President of Loyola University, Chicago, an appointment that was seen as a splendid opportunity for an accomplished and solid scholar of mathematics, philosophy and theology. Loyola was, at that time, the wealthiest and most complex of America's Jesuit institutions, with graduate schools in medicine, law, business, nursing, theology, social work and education. Their medical center had largely carried the university forward since it opened in 1969, but recent cutbacks in Medicare and managed-care organizations were taking their toll, seriously eroding its income. In earlier years, the medical center had annual net incomes of nearly $40 million, and this cash cow was also propping up various other programs across its campus. But now, the university was running increasingly on borrowed time, and its development operation was simply not up to the challenge.

Despite Loyola's sizable endowment, there had been little focus on institutional development. Consequently, its enrollment continued to slide, by 12 percent in 2000, even though its main Chicago competitor, DePaul University, achieved a 19 percent increase over the same period. By that time, Loyola faced deficits of $140 million, forcing tuitions to escalate by nearly 75 percent. Its endowment had lost nearly 30 percent of it value. The university, therefore, was forced in 1995 to hive off its medical center—its main source of revenues. Four years later, Piderit let go another 36 faculty and staff members, triggering a movement to have him removed. He resigned in June, 2001.

What lessons can be learned from this experience? For one thing, Loyola had failed to reinvent itself, and to focus more on the bread-and-butter business of undergraduate education. Their top team failed to see the trends that were clearly showing a fall in enrollments, while they retained an excess of faculty and staff to support the diminishing student body. Also, two-thirds of Loyola's revenue had come from tuitions, meaning that enrollment management should have been the top priority. Loyola's response to this impending debacle was to cut back on the proliferation of degree offerings. But despite experimenting with various patches, it was too late. Had Loyola been a commercial organization, it would have had the business skills to make the right course corrections well ahead of the disaster that eventually unfolded.

There are many other similar situations across the US. Most state legislatures have not been able to maintain public funding commensurate with cost increases. Each year there are more mergers and closures among small liberal colleges. During the decade 1995 to 2005, only some 40 percent of the nation's colleges described their financial conditions as "excellent" or "very good"; a dismal report card.

Indeed, some say that the wolf is not just at the door, but that it is already inside, in the guise of budget reductions, rising costs, unfriendly legislation and competition from the for-profit sector.[47] Richard Alfred, Associate Professor of Education at the University of Michigan, says that the fodder which the wolf craves includes security, pride, lack of a team ethos, immunity from lapses of accountability, resistance to change and other familiar attitudes. He sees academia as growing ever more fragile, and that the best time for any organization to change is while it is still successful. Yet colleges and universities are designed, by tradition, for futures that avoid needed change. The steps on the path that lead from success to struggle are:

1. Lack of Urgency

Lessening of quality, trust and community that defeats the goal of having an efficient (let alone an optimal) organization. The cost of this is incalculable. Process cycles of real change are getting ever shorter; from about seven years a decade ago, to nearly three now. The implications for academia are both significant and unprecedented.

2. Limited Staff Engagement

Faculty carries heavier workloads than ever, and toils under ever-tightening space and administrative support. Yet they are expected to keep up with students, new technologies and content delivery. The public face is moving toward being less visible, friendly and understanding.

---

47. "The Wolf at the Door: Where Colleges Could Fail," an article by Richard Alfred, Associate Professor of Education, the University of Michigan, in the *Community College Journal*, April/May 2003, pp. 16-24.

3. Imbedded Culture

The academic community fosters subcultures which are growing ever fractious by age and social generation group, by basis of employment, and by narrower domains of responsibility.

4. Value

Traditional academia is no longer the sole cradle of learning in higher education. Its mission is increasingly splintered by the steady inroads of corporate and for-profit universities which are threatening the traditional role of institutions. Value now has two different faces: economic, and enrichment. The good news is that modern technologies are now offering learning in any way, in any place, and at any time. The bad news is that it is making learning more impersonal and isolated, and less collaborative.

5. Management Perspective

Leadership and perspective has become much more important. Leadership is molded by accumulated experience, and not merely taught. There is also a greater need to create and sustain a sense of caring, ownership and community, along with setting organizational processes and developing responsible fiscal skills.

As mentioned previously, the business of higher education is as challenging as any, if not more so. Tuitions and fees through the decade of the '90s generally tripled at state and private universities. And the recession in the first years of the 21st century has led to many programs being cut or merged in the interest of economy and competitiveness. Mergers and closures are at all-time highs. A merger, after all, is a last-ditch effort to retain some of the college's identity and heritage, lest the gates slam shut for good. But even this big step is not always successful in preserving the best of what an institution has stood for.

Small private liberal arts colleges across the country have to take it on the chin. Typically under endowed, some of these institutions have, for three centuries, been stalwarts of the higher educational system. But in recent times they have been closing their doors at an alarming rate. In the last 13 years more than 100 four-year colleges have closed their doors (while the number of corporate universities has ballooned from 400 to more than 3,500). Faced with rising expectations among all ranks, students, faculty and administrative staff are all struggling under the burdens of rising salaries, competition for faculty, increasing operating expenses and the higher expectations of students for more and better amenities. Yet some see the future more optimistically. It is possible that some closures could be avoided by alliances and mergers, such as DePaul University's (failed) absorption of Chicago's Barat College. Are these mere precursors of many others yet to follow? These consolidations make economic sense, and are on the upswing.

There are several factors at work which might undermine the stability of small liberal arts colleges. Among them are:

- Students are increasingly mobile and are willing to move away to better known, more prestigious colleges.
- State institutions are organizing themselves into clusters of honor colleges, to provide the small-college ambiance and experience that students want.
- There is increasing competition from public institutions reaching across state borders to tap into a larger pool of good students.
- The desire for job-specific programs rather than only a liberal arts education is greater.
- And more women are going to college. Some coed institutions have enrolled more women than men. Typically under endowed, these institutions have long been the stalwarts of the system, but they are now faced with rising expectations. Still, the future can be viewed optimistically.

The figures below are taken from the US Census Bureau projections for 2005. All figures are in millions:

Number of Students, by Gender			
	Full time	Part time	Total
Male Students Enrolled	4.361	2.624	6.985
Female Students Enrolled	5.254	3.896	9.150
Total Students Enrolled	9.615	6.520	16.135

Number of Students, by Private & Public Institutions			
	Public Institutions	Private Institutions	Total
4-year	6.509	3.474	9.933
2-year	5.879	273.000	6.152
Total Students Enrolled	12.388	276.474	16.135

Colleges, especially those smaller schools that are struggling to compete with the large and powerful, need to look for alignments and collaborations in order to become vigorous and self-sustaining. Sharing information technologies among smaller, close-by institutions can be a lifesaver. It is simply too costly for small private and public institutions to go it alone, each carrying the cost burden of complex IT systems and related administration. Those that will prevail in the long term are those that actively seek formal collaborations and become partners with other proximate colleges and universities for mutual gain. They can reinvent their institutions.

What are the implications of these inevitable pressures of change? Smaller colleges will struggle to keep admissions affordable at traditional levels. State legislatures of public institutions are finding it ever harder to fund them adequately. A new mantra of public higher education is about making the transition from being state supported, to state assisted, and inevitability to the state *located* school. Although state institutions continue to be the main source of funding of higher education across the nation, their share continues to shrink. This trend further shifts the educational burden from taxpayers to corporations and wealthy alums.

Successful mergers are those that share common, core heritages. Candidate institutions tend be small, face financial problems because of declining enrollments, and lack strong alumni associations. They often are not widely known and lack national or international reputations, but may share religious or other common heritages. Generally, they are physically proximate to each other. This was the case in New York's Westchester County when Marymount College consolidated with Fordham University.

However, DePaul University's acquisition of Barat College, a Roman Catholic women's college on Chicago's wealthy North Shore, did not go so well. The case is instructive because of the complexity of issues that play into such deals. DePaul quickly came to see Barat as a drain on resources, and consequently decided to divest itself of the college only one year after the merger. By then the team of administrators who had conceived the merger had left. The new administrators did not share their vision; they were deterred by the fact that it would be expensive to maintain and upgrade the Barat campus appropriately. Instead, they wanted to concentrate their efforts and resources in Lincoln Park, near the heart of Chicago's inner city. Ultimately, a buyer came in to seal the deal; the wealthy suburban area it served, in Lake Forest, was growing. DePaul had misjudged the market opportunity.

Mergers between colleges and universities need not be win-lose transactions. On the contrary, they can bring valuable synergies.[48] Stanford and Harvard have recently been close to a merger of parts of their respective b-school operations. The bold plan was to combine executive MBA programs to market the combined brand and make it a for-profit entity that would extend its reach worldwide. The joint venture would have, from the outset, revenues of more than $100 million available for program development and operations. Harvard would bring its strengths in general management and leadership; Stanford would offer a reputation in entrepreneurship, e-commerce and innovation. Other mergers have been sought between the Columbia Business School and London Business School, and The University of Pennsylvania with Wharton and France's INSEAD. According to Laura D'Andrea Tyson, former Dean of the University of California at Berkeley's Haas School of Business, "This will only intensify this trend and force our hands."

As minority students make up a larger proportion of students seeking higher education, a growing number of them are choosing for-profit colleges. At least half of the enrollment at DeVry, ITT Technical Institute, and Strayer University—all of which have numerous campuses across the United States—is in minority students. In 2003, Sylvan shed

---

48. "When Harvard Met Stanford," in *Business Week*, April 30, 2001, p. 46.

its elementary and secondary education facilities to focus instead on its online education and its network of international universities. They intend to build a postsecondary education company to eventually serve some 200,000 students. Sylvan already has campuses in Chile, France, Mexico, Spain and Switzerland. These and other for-profits focus more on the basic skills needed in the marketplace, and less on intellectual pursuits.

The advent of for-profit competitors in the academic arena has raised many new issues of interest to the Federal government. In particular, such institutions are interested in amending the Higher Education Act, to change the definition of "higher education institution" in order to include these colleges and to make them eligible for Federal funding. In addition, for-profit colleges are asking Congress to:

- Require colleges to publish annual reports that would measure their success in the retention and graduation of students and in career preparation.
- Eliminate the requirement that for-profit institutions earn at least 10 percent of their revenue from sources other than Federal student aid to remain eligible to participate in the government's aid programs.
- Rewrite a provision that makes it difficult for the for-profit institutions to challenge, in Federal court, actions taken by the US Education Department. Officials say these institutions need a due process to stop the Department from taking steps that they believe to be unlawful or arbitrary and capricious.
- Ease the rule under which colleges that enroll more than half of their students via distance education cannot offer Federal student aid.

Traditional colleges and universities are indeed quite different from the private and nonprofit sectors in several important aspects. Among them is their difficulty in responding quickly to shifting economics and markets. They simply cannot add or cut faculty quickly, if needed. Instead, they must do a superior job at improving strategic planning and business processes if they are to compete successfully. This is an area in which most college presidents generally are not expert. Some have an instinct for it; some have consultants to advise them, and others simply do it clumsily or not at all.

These are interesting times. According to the Education Commission of the States, traditional private two-year colleges continue to be threatened, and continue to close their doors at a rate of about three percent each year. However, four-year institutions, at least for the time being, continue to multiply. During the period 1989-2000 non-profit colleges and universities increased by 613, or about 3 percent. And in the same period private colleges increased by 4 percent to 1,526. As for the four-year for-profit institutions, during the same time period, our traditional colleges grew as shown:

Non-profit	Increased by 4%, to 1,526
For-profit	Increased by 266%, to 194

Altogether, during the 1990s, the for-profit sector increased enrollment by 59 percent, or some 366,000 students. For-profit, degree-granting institutions continue to grow significantly faster than their nonprofit counterparts. In the decade beginning 1990, 4-year, for-profit institutions grew by 194, against 613 for nonprofits.

Ralph Bradburd of Williams College, a scholar of corporate mergers, sees many possible advantages to collegiate consolidations. He notes that many of the redundant services offered by other colleges' administrations, such as accounting, plant maintenance and registrations, could be combined. Such mergers could reduce marketing costs, and might allow newly merged entities to charge more tuition because they would no longer have to compete on price with close rivals. Furthermore, a combined institution could sell off any underutilized space and assets, and save further by having larger classes, which would be possible because it would be drawing from a bigger pool of students.

With all the emphasis on mergers, there is a very different approach to building institutional strength which must not be overlooked. The small Muskingum College in New Concord, Ohio was on the ropes, financially. Their remedy was simple: cut tuitions and fees by nearly 30 percent. This enabled them to increase enrollments. The students loved it, and the faculty and staff found ways to reduce costs further. A decade later, the college is thriving. It had been doing all the traditional things that incrementally-driven administrators use to plan for each year ahead.

But this College took a longer view and had the courage to commit to a serious and fundamental makeover of itself and its future.[49]

Some authorities have developed various criteria for measuring the vulnerability of small and weak institutions. Richard Ekman, President of the 490-member Council of Independent Colleges, says that any school with fewer than 3,000 students is especially vulnerable. He encourages such institutions to consolidate functions and activities whenever practical: information systems; purchasing, such as in meals supplies; sharing library resources; outsourcing functions such as accounting and payroll; and services such as vending, laundry, parking and security. Gordon Winston, a professor of political economy affiliated with the Williams College Project on the Economics of Higher Education, says that recent research shows that the break-even point for many small colleges is about 1,800 students, unless the college has a large endowment such as Williams. Other observers see different figures, and only time will tell how serious the institutional shake-up will be. The only point of consensus is that it is coming, and approaching fast.[50]

An inspirational example of how a small, low-profile private institution had the wisdom and courage to reinvent itself and transform radically its basic business model can be found in Bellevue University, Nebraska.[51] President John Muller set out to reinvent his university by rethinking its business model and taking only the best elements of its for-profit counterparts, but remaining nonprofit. This was his game plan:

- Focus on getting students out of school and into jobs in 3 or 3.5 years, for adult students are more focused. Students want degrees that directly plug into job opportunities.
- Keep their roots in core series of courses on "American vision and values."
- Spend 10 percent of budget on marketing: radio, TV and billboards.
- Plan to expand into other markets in the upper Midwest.

---

49. "Slashing Prices Draws a Crowd," in The Chronicle of Higher Education, August 1, 2003.
50. "More Colleges are Seeing the Virtues of Merging," in The Chronicle of Higher Education, March 23, 2001, pp. A26-30.
51. "Acting Like a For-Profit College," in The Chronicle of Higher Education, August 1, 2003, p. A24.

- Be competitive within community colleges by keeping tuition low. "Our administration is constantly looking for ways to cut costs. It has set a goal of raising the ratio of students to administrators to 40:1 from 30:1 in next four years." With costs so low, operating margins just keep growing.
- No tenure. Full-time faculty members comprise 22 percent of the entire teaching staff, so there are many part-timers who work under one-, two- or three-year contracts. Thus, they can operate between traditional institutions and the for-profit institutions. "We're not 100 percent adjunct-driven like Phoenix, nor are we like Phoenix."

In this same spirit, the Chicago City Colleges (CCC) decided in 1995 to outsource their counselors and accountants. These jobs can often be done just as well and at lower cost in the private sector. Moreover, the institution is not burdened by carrying employees during cycles when the workloads slow down, and has more flexibility to bring in temporary staff when work intensifies, such as in the autumn of each year. In the CCC system, counselors are regarded in the same manner as faculty members, and therefore have the same collective bargaining power as the faculty. This particular system—and others as well—is even now experimenting with the outsourcing of certain faculty members. This is in keeping with the ever-increasing proportion of adjunct "for hire" instructors.

There are usually pay differentials between schools in universities. Business school professors are typically paid more than those in the humanities, for instance; engineering more than nursing. Compensation is always a tricky balance between fairness and equity on the one hand, and supply and market forces on the other. Colleges and universities are constantly confronted with these dilemmas, in good times and in bad. For example, average salaries in Medicine in 2004 were about $188,000; $109,000 in Law; $95,000 in the Basic Sciences; and $88,000 in Business.

Academia could also do a much better job by instituting quality processes. Most efforts to improve quality processes are focused internally. Many fail to look outside of the institution, to see how competitors are operating. What are their visions and aspirations? What initiatives are they planning for in order to improve their programs, rankings and financial positions? These institutions would be well-advised to engage in benchmarking projects that will determine, objectively, just how they compare. The wider business community has generally succeeded in this. Other opportunities for improvement are outlined below.

Firstly, with very few exceptions, campuses across America simply languish during the summer months. Some use this time to attract various groups for study, and faculty members use it to concentrate on their research programs and other non-educational pursuits. But college campuses could offer space and facilities during summer months for industrialists and other working professionals to interact, network and devote time to planning and strategy, away from the normal fray. Rather than let these facilities lie dormant for those months, they could increase the utilization of these facilities, for economic gain. Make the facilities available for academic and executive programs, for teacher training, and to special groups such as high school students and senior citizens.

Secondly, Northwestern University's McCormick School of Engineering has developed a novel way to enhance partnerships with industrial companies. *FastScience* was created to make it easy and inexpensive for manufacturers to get tests and evaluations done within the University. Its intent is to provide on-the-spot, pre-packaged testing for small jobs, thus circumventing the more tedious processes of the Office of Grants and Contracts.

This service has been a breakthrough for small companies lacking sophisticated capabilities internally. FastScience provides the client with a single point of contact, generally delivering results in no more than two working days, with unbiased data and opinions. It is streamlined, using generic contracts. There are no proposals, and little or no intellectual property issues. The client can be there to witness the testing evaluation, in real time. Typical services include materials evaluations and testing, x-ray diffraction, tribology, modeling and simulation, process optimization, database creation and related projects. FastScience provides easy access to academe by affording rapid service to industry, while enabling the university to utilize its capital assets better and to expand its research programs. It might become a research template for institutions to use to the benefit of both academia and industry.

Moreover, schools like the University of Chicago's Great Minds program offer evening and weekend programs for any and all who simply want to continue to keep themselves intellectually alive. It is good for the community and for facility utilization. Southwestern University in Georgetown, Texas, a small liberal arts college more than 150 years old, offers a wide range of lectures and short courses under their Senior University program.

Big money is now pouring into the education business,[52] but it is still too soon to tell the magnitude of the payoff. Fueled by reform efforts and students who have grown up with the Internet, more schools and universities are moving course work and communication onto the Web. Professor Billie Wright Dziech at the University of Cincinnati says that distance learning has a growing place and a significant future in delivering higher education to certain segments of the population. But it is not for all students. Furthermore, cost-cutting corporations are turning more and more to distance e-Learning as a more efficient means of upgrading employee skills. According to Merrill Lynch, the knowledge-enterprise industry now stands at some $735 billion, and includes spending on a host of things including textbooks, software and services. And it will only grow larger.

The United States Congress is another important source of funding. But some of this is earmarked to specific institutions without competition. These governmental expenses have been tracked and it has been found that the bill to the taxpayers exceeds $2 billion a year. Such funding generally is noncompetitive and there is rapid growth, both in the number of institutions benefiting (more than 700) and the bill to taxpayer.

The e-learning, lifetime learning market is soaring. Industry seeks to use educational technology to improve employee skills, investing in human capital while saving time and money. Industrial companies are increasing their training programs aggressively, because it pays off handsomely. Motorola Corp.'s corporate training branch, Motorola Uni-

---

52. From "e-Commerce Overview: The Hope, and the Reality," in the Wall Street Journal, March 12, 2001, p. R6.

versity, is a case in point. Nearly 30 percent of Motorola's employee training has taken place on the web. The $30 billion Chicago giant estimates that employees can complete a course on the Web in five hours, down from eight in a traditional instructor-led classroom, and it expects the time savings to become even greater. This means that Motorola, which requires a minimum of 40 hours a year in training for all new employees, can now more than triple the amount of learning its employees receive. It is all about learning better, faster and continuously; and all integrated within workers' normal duties.

Motorola has identified five skills that teachers and administrators must focus on to create the "worker of the future." These skills can be the focus not just of adult learners, but of any primary or secondary school system. They are:

• **Language/communication skills**: the ability to read and write; to comprehend and easily use a wide range of printed materials; and to speak clearly and effectively. This is a growing need in American industry.

• **Quantitative skills**: the ability to perform basic mathematical computations, to understand charts and graphs, and to apply these skills in analyzing synthesized and quantitative data.

• **Problem-solving skills**: the ability to reason and to solve practical problems, to follow complex written or oral instructions, and to deal with situations in which there may be several variables.

• **Interpersonal/attitudinal skills**: possession of qualities of self-esteem, motivation, reliability and punctuality, the ability to deal with and work cooperatively with others, and acceptance of the concepts of lifelong learning, uncertainty, and change.

• **Job-seeking/self-advancement skills**: the capacity to assess one's abilities and ambitions and to cultivate the skills needed to fulfill those ambitions.

The power to change and continually strengthen these five skills needs to be shared with the local school councils, parent-teacher organizations and school boards.

The intrusion of corporations into America's traditional higher academic market has signaled a big change in educational culture. For example, Hewlett-Packard funds some 500 students and faculty in ten selected colleges and universities around the world. Motorola and other large, technology-driven companies are doing likewise.

Academia has to draw up new rules in dealing with companies that seek access to their faculty and intellectual capital. MIT, one of the great entrepreneurial universities, has five basic rules regarding the process of launching new ventures:

- All MIT research must be university-initiated.
- Everything must be publishable right away, or within the time it takes to file patent applications.
- Industry pays full institutional overheard costs.
- MIT will do no confidential research, although it will keep confidential any business-related information on request.
- Faculty and students that create new businesses may not do so on MIT property.

This is a very fair and disciplined approach to managing a university's intellectual property.

As corporations seek to become more important players in academia regarding continuing education and other linkages, they will increasingly expect to have a say in what is being taught, and how. This issue is addressed in part by industrial advisory groups and similar boards to colleges. Often, however, industrial members are little more than social delegates in this, and have no real authority to improve or change issues of real consequence. These advisory groups generally focus simply on a *quid pro quo* platform in which the academics get access to equipment, and the industrialists get access to good students. These shallow partnerships will undoubtedly deepen in the years ahead.

Historically, teaching and academic research have made for attractive careers for many people. Some were "born" to the profession. However, the profession is changing ever faster. Some find the academic field to be more uncomfortable than before, and choose to drop out to pursue other vocations. Across the nation, increasing numbers of top PhDs in the field are opting out of academe, to take up other commercial careers which are less stressful and pay more. This can be risky, and stepping off the academic track has its own perils. One usually has but a single opportunity to make this switch, and it is rare to return after snubbing academia. Robert J. Sternberg, a professor of psychology at Yale University, says that being a professor does not carry the prestige of a physician. His advice is that "Academics are for people who really love it. Otherwise, it's really a bad job."

A cornerstone of the modern research university is the recognition that knowledge is an economic asset. This leads institutions to chase research for its funding and revenues. It provides for the luster of brand imaging. This may have begun with Jean-Jacques Rousseau in 1761, when he argued that knowledge is "a species of money, which is valued greatly, but that only adds to our well-being in proportion as it is communicated, and is only good in commerce." In modern times, the Bayh-Dole Act of 1980 allowed universities to own rights to government-funded research conducted within their walls. According to Lita Nelsen, Director of MIT's Technology Licensing Office, this had the effect of bringing inventions out of the laboratory and more quickly into the public domain. This Act also has a secondary benefit in that colleges and universities can go to industry and offer it access to new government-inspired technology, because universities now had royalty-bearing licenses. She says, "The university could continue to do basic science and develop embryonic ideas as they always had, but now industry can run with the risks of the marketplace."

Nelsen also warns of the potential for conflicts of interest that could pit economic gains against research integrity. She notes that "When a company pays for a researcher's time, almost all aspects of research can be adjusted to conform with corporate expectations: design studies, methodology execution, analysis, enrollment of research subjects, peer review, publication and dissemination of results." Biomedical researchers are increasingly being funded directly by pharmaceutical companies. And there is a falloff in published research among university researchers having close industry ties. Gross revenues from such licenses represent, on average, less than three percent of all R&D funding from US universities. Thus, this concern has not yet risen to the level of misuse—but clearly calls for oversight.

A further, unique element of academia is its network of academic presses. This is a group of some 150 independent university-related publishing companies which span the globe, although most are located in North America. These small enterprises are part of the Association of American University Presses (AAUP, but not to be confused with the American Association of University Professors, which uses the same acronym). Quartered in New York City, this non-profit organization has the mission to support works of scholarly, intellectual or creative merit, often for small audiences of specialists. The AAUP has long played an important role in publishing, but its mission is in need of renewal.

Originally conceived for publishing doctoral research, these presses unfortunately no longer play the important intellectual role that they once did. In the past they afforded young and senior academics a way to publish books of modest market interest, often helping junior professors in attaining tenure. Growth rates of books from these presses have plummeted to historic lows, because the nature of scholarly books has long been shunned by a book-buying public that does not value these particular products. As a result, academic presses face eroding markets and sales, and rising costs.

Except for the MIT Press and a few others, most university presses have largely been aimed at the social sciences and humanities, and not at the pure and applied sciences. But this, too, is changing as the market for humanities books is shrinking and the sciences and engineering fields are finding their way more into the academic presses. But because most editors of university presses are, themselves, not trained and experienced in technology, they have not, until recently, welcomed these manuscripts. Sir C.P. Snow, the famous novelist, physicist and British government officer, said it for the ages: "Closing the gap between our cultures (the arts and the sciences) is a necessity in the most abstract intellectual sense as well as in the most practical. When those two senses grow apart, then no society is going to be able to think with wisdom." It is the responsibility and the mission of the university presses to help reunite these two factions.

Clearly, then, the book market is changing, and these presses must adapt. "The scholarly monograph is dead," says Kenneth Arnold, former Director of the Rutgers University Press. He says books today must be aimed at larger markets, and not just at community service. Book runs have always been small, but now are getting ever smaller—typically less than 1,000 copies—although some have broader appeal and, therefore, do somewhat better.

The salvation for the university presses must be in moving away from producing only scholarly monographs for libraries, and toward books that have broader appeal, so as to compete with commercial bookstores. This approach has the potential to increase average print runs by some ten to twenty times current volumes. Another path is for university presses to open themselves to non-academics that have something important to say both to academics and non-academics. These publishers can survive only if they can become more than just academic publishers. But the best therapy may be to turn to virtual books and manuscripts that can be self-published online. This new medium is growing and developing quite rapidly. Books "printed" by this medium are generally subject to all the customary quality standards, and are being regarded as legitimate publications. And many traditional publishers now also offer their printed works in audio formats.

Here is a summary of the problems and issues facing university presses.[53]

- Library budgets have shifted dramatically toward science and technology journals and large expensive databases. These presses have less and less budgets for books. As one market diminishes, another avenue has to be found to replace it.
- University administrators have come to assume that a university press must pay for books that lose money by publishing those that make money.
- Academic authors in the past made marketing a more important reason for choosing a press than the vital quality aspects of refereeing, editing, or proofreading.

---

53. "5 Problems and 9 Solutions for University Presses," in *The Chronicle of Higher Education*, June 13, 2003, pp. B7-B9.

- Influential donors like the Andrew W. Mellon Foundation, as well as university libraries and administrators, have long pressured university presses to move rapidly toward electronic publishing. But this could further sap press budgets, strain press staffs, and demoralize press directors, all of whom are struggling to keep their boats afloat. Also, book authors still prefer to see their works in traditional bound products, rather than in softcopy.
- Trade publishers, in response to a 1979 Supreme Court decision that commercial inventory is taxable, sharply reduced their inventories by licensing rights to hundreds of books to university presses. They were happy to reap the profits from books that sold only a few hundred copies year after year. And scholars will continue to buy books in fields they cherish.

Some of the solutions offered are:

- Authors need to take more care to write clearly and concisely, so that books are less expensive, more valuable and more readable.
- Authors and publishers alike should pay as much attention to design and editing as they do to "market splash".
- University administrations must care enough to invest in their university presses up front, either paying for the costs of electronic publishing or ceasing to expect it.
- Presses should care enough to befriend librarians and scientists—their customers.
- When a university press is in trouble, faculty members, especially in the humanities and social sciences, should fight the good fight to continue to support their curricula.

3. THE COST STRUCTURE AND ECONOMICS OF HIGHER EDUCATION

Derek Bok, President Emeritus of Harvard University, states that all institutions of higher education must be vigilant in watching for ethical "slippery slopes" that can compromise academic integrity. College and university administrators today are under great pressure to become more entrepreneurial. And profiting is good, until it reaches the point where it can be a deterrent to improving academic work and higher education's value to society. Here are Bok's five steps to mitigating such ethical dilemmas:

1. Do not rely solely on presidents to protect the institution and its values from the dangers of commercialization. They have also to tend to

fundraising, faculty and student development, and other needs that compete for scarce resources.

2. Do not consider implementing commercial opportunities without an ethical framework for guidance. Institutions should insist on having a set of rules to deal with current issues such as secrecy provisions in corporate research agreements, admissions standards for athletes, and conflicts of interest for scientists. Ad hoc decisions can lead to a gradual erosion of academic values, and the institution will always pay the freight.

3. Faculty governance is not perfect, but do not end-run difficult decisions, leaving them to be made by administrators simply because of the time and effort needed to engage the voice of the faculty. Rather, put in place effective procedures; use sub-committees that are competent in the specific issues at hand, such as secrecy and emerging opportunities.

4. Create policies that cover difficult issues such as conflicts of interest in research, the window of time for which commercial research findings can be kept secret, conference-wide rules protecting academic standards in athletics, and many other such matters.

5. Higher educational institutions are, like those in the private sector, subject to abrupt changes in income streams. Stability is important to both sectors, and a steady erosion of support over an extended period of time can put intolerable pressures on universities to sacrifice important academic standards in the hope of gaining badly needed revenue through compromising commercial ventures.

These are crucial tests of leadership. Ultimately, colleges and universities have to be seen for what they are: large and complex enterprises which require professional management. Chancellors and presidents, deans and faculties must accept the fact that their job is to lead boldly and thoughtfully. And one of the first steps in leadership is to create and use specific measurable plans that draw the line on expenses, while finding ways to do things differently and with commitment to serve their various constituencies. Academic institutions generally have not implemented bold, farsighted strategies aimed at making themselves stronger. Schools have not been sufficiently reinvented so that they can operate efficiently in modern times. The comfortable and nostalgic images of schools operating leisurely, with bankers' hours and summers off, persist.

As indicated previously, many colleges and universities have to downsize, even as enrollments have continued to grow. US universities employ about 15 percent fewer tenured professors than they did in 1985. Faculties faithfully protect their rights regarding traditional continuing tenure. Administrators see it from still a different perspective, as will be seen later in this chapter. Along with this, institutions which recruit and train faculty members, and who equip them to use new educational technologies should provide better learning at less cost. Anything less should be unacceptable.

There is a confluence of four interrelated forces that will inevitably remold higher education: costs, demographics, market consolidations and greater expectations of total educational quality delivered. There are three factions at play within each and every institution: students, faculty and the staff. Intersecting with these factions is the need to better engage teaching, service and research funding obligations—all for the betterment of students (customers). There has always been an undercurrent of divisiveness and tension between faculty and administrative staff. This suboptimal behavior robs the institution of energy and trust. Of course, there will always be differences of opinion, but a real team will accommodate compromises for the greater good of long-term excellence. Therefore, the work of the trustees and senior officers of the institution must be to learn how to lead, and how to compromise. In the long term, effective leadership will ameliorate the bumps on the road, and make for a better future.

The task of nourishing eager minds is far from being perfected. Educational costs in the US continue to outpace inflation rates, threefold. How can this be? How could any market get away with such runaway cost escalations for decades, unchallenged by others and with a relatively low cost structure? The answer lies in the traditional slow-to-change culture of academia. But just as nature abhors a vacuum, the ways of traditional academia are facing serious competition in the explosive growth of for-profit colleges and universities, as discussed earlier. This development will be explored later in this chapter.

There follows a summary of the infrastructure of colleges and universities (2000 data):

- Community Colleges:

    1,101 in number

    5.7 million enrollments

    Cost of educating a student: $5K—$9K

- Public Four-Year Colleges:

    612 in number

    4.8 million enrollments

    $4,081 tuition

    47 percent get bachelor degree within 5 years

- Private Colleges:

    1,676 in number

    2.2 million enrollments

    $18,273 average tuition

    $12—$80K to educate a student

    62 percent get bachelor degree within 5 years

- For-Profit Colleges:

    808 in number

    403,000 enrollments

    $11,043 average tuition

    1 percent gets BAs within 5 years.

Endowments and Business Planning

Endowments are vital to all traditional colleges and universities, private or public. They do not create wealth, as do other companies. Rather, they need outside money sources in order to operate and for buildings and grounds, equipment, professorships and other necessities. Endowments provide the institutional "flywheel" that propels a school ahead, toward a future vision. Right or wrong, the outside world measures an institution by its endowment.

There has always been individual and corporate gifting to higher educational institutions. The need for it is foremost in the minds of faculty and administrators. In troubled times and economic downturns, personal and institutional priorities and decisions must be reexamined against earlier practices. And when state deficits capture the headlines across the nation, the mood for sustained giving from companies and individuals abates. Giving by alumni—especially of undesignated gifts—dries up quickly. Colleges and universities then have a very difficult job juggling endowments and other funds. Development officers and other fundraisers also have a serious and difficult charge: to bring in money, both in good times and in bad. They do best when using an integrated approach which creates teams for marketing, information, and services, and to cultivate long-term relations with alumni, and institutional donors.

And what about the private sources of funding? In 1980 gifts and endowments made up about 3 percent of all costs; twenty years later it had risen to 7 percent. And most of these private sources go to private schools, many of which are quite comfortable.

A small minority of elite private universities have substantial endowments and therefore are somewhat immunized from the impact of economic swings, as contrasted with the majority of public institutions. But the great majority of America's private colleges and universities lack resources, and struggle to balance the books while still offering an affordable, world-class educational experience.

Harvard University leads the list in institutional endowments, with $18.8 billion (year 2004). After Harvard come Yale ($12.7 billion), The University of Texas System ($10.3 billion), Stanford ($9.9 billion), Princeton ($9.0 billion), MIT ($5.9 billion), the University of California System ($4.8 billion), Emory ($4.5 billion), Columbia University ($4.5 billion), and the Texas A&M University System ($4.4 billion). The mean institutional endowment is only about $72 million, and many schools operate on the thin edge of solvency.

Along with efforts to fortify colleges and universities, institutional endowments have long been soaring. Once making only a modest effort to raise funds for caretaker needs, colleges and universities now have well-oiled, professional foundation staffs to build endowments. More than 40 US institutions have endowments in excess of $1 billion. Until recently, these endowments have realized average rates of return of more than 18 percent a year, and that figure is rising. But the new millennium ushered in an era of reduced giving and diminished portfolio values. State appropriations for higher education are also shrinking, heralding a spate of faculty and staff layoffs, salary freezes and cuts, and the elimination of fringe academic programs.

Financial institutes are warning colleges against taking risky investment strategies and using too much endowment income to cover their operating costs and debt service. Fitch IBCA, a rater of college bond services, cautions that institutions with endowments larger than $500M tend to invest substantial portions of their money in alternative assets like venture capital funds, hedge funds and managed futures. Colleges with endowments of $1B or more tend to invest about 30 percent of their funds in such assets, while those with endowments of $500M—$1B have invested only 18 percent of their endowments in that way. Moreover, colleges which rely heavily upon endowment income for operating expenses are not regarded as favorably as those with multiple source funds. Analysts do not want to see institutions use too much of their endowment to retire debt. Institutions will do well for their students if they can use their endowments to discount student tuitions and fees. This strategy also enables institutions to be even more selective in choosing their students and faculty. In the final analysis, schools that save better than others will move up the ladder; the rest will move down.

Administrators need to take a leaf from the private sector and develop long-term (five years or more) business plans. Such planning has the following components:
- Funds for new and stronger programs; and offload of the weak
- Preparation for contingencies and risks
- Attention to macroeconomic forecasts
- Awareness of competition from new for-profit institutions
- Demographics
- Management of infrastructural needs
- Promotion of brand

Entrepreneurship

Economic volatility in higher education will continue. Because colleges and universities cannot hire and fire employees as easily as can other institutions, they will need more effective strategies and policies to keep their institutions afloat during hard economic times. State legislators will need to muster the discipline not to cut taxes in good times, only to struggle later on. As an example, the State of Washington is packaging its spending plans as economic development plans, to be used to raise additional funds which can offset tuitions and fund new initiatives.

College administrators will have to lobby even harder for more state and local funds. Success will be achieved when the focus is on better and more efficient ways of educating the nation—ways that are more cost-effective, and have programs that are truly relevant to contemporary times.

In this era of economic malaise, state legislatures typically see higher education budgets as somewhat discretionary, and thus to be trimmed when needed. This was witnessed with the advent of the millennium recession, when many public institutions, such as the Universities of Massachusetts, Iowa, Missouri and Texas, were forced to increase tuitions by over 20 percent a year. A common goal should be to set tuitions that are visible, in line with competitors, and that are geared to cover actual costs.

Unfortunately, state commitments to public higher education seem to be getting softer with time. State universities' operating budgets are generally less than 25 percent of the entire costs required. The rest comes from government and private sector funding, gifts, and other sources. In 1980 state spending was 63 percent of educational and general revenues. By 2000 it had fallen to 51 percent, and continues along this trend.[54] State legislatures have also been cutting their share of dollars earmarked for public colleges: from 9.8 percent in 1980, to 6.9 percent in 2000; and the trend continues.

---

54. "As Tuitions Rise, What Will Happen to Quality and Access?," in *The* Chronicle of Higher Education, Sept.19, 2003, pp. B7-B11.

Colleges and universities, challenged as they are by ever higher costs, must continually find ways to raise new and additional funding, and cut costs. Expenditures on computer security, health care, new construction and various kinds of debt service are on the rise. To balance these increases, institutions are finding it necessary to pull back on electronic learning systems and general maintenance. This is a worry.

Still another way to manage the spiraling costs of education is to keep annual increases within tight boundaries. In the few states that use biennial budgeting, state officials can somewhat dampen such rapid increases, and smooth them out. Another approach, used in Missouri and other states, is to link tuitions to some official index, such as a consumer price index.

Despite all the good news, the task of higher education is getting ever more challenging. On the revenue side, there is a fall in state appropriations and Federal grants, and more dependence upon foreign nationals. Deficits can only be offset by the need to increase revenues in the form of rising tuitions and investment returns. But on the plus side, fundraising is on the rise. Each year private and public institutions launch and complete capital campaigns in billions of dollars. Such campaigns are tricky to complete successfully, and college and university foundations know that this is a capricious business.

Institutions are finding that they must work harder than ever to identify new and effective targets for cost cutting. Here are some typical examples of innovations.[55]

- Purdue University consolidated food service and dining hall operations, making them more customer friendly.
- Knox College adopted a "use it or lose it" and a "trusting" approach to budgeting.
- The University of Michigan cut 20 vehicles from its fleet.
- Whittier College removed 50 percent of light bulbs in some fluorescent fixtures.
- Eastern Illinois University reduced thermostats in buildings by 2 degrees, down to 68 degrees

---

55. "6 Creative Ways Colleges are Cutting Costs," in *The Chronicle of Higher Education*, Dec. 6, 2002, pp. A27-A28.

- Michigan Technological University restructured its health insurance plan by charging co-payments for some services that were once free; users pay a monthly fee for their health-care plan, and have switched co-payment amounts from a flat fee to a percentage of the cost of the service.

It must be recognized that some areas and disciplines differ in their imbedded costs of education delivery. For example, the cost of undergraduate education varies according to discipline, and is less costly than graduate education. Engineering programs are more expensive than Liberal Arts; and Medicine is more expensive than Business, which implies that different programs and curricula cost more to serve. This fact has led some administrators to levy tuition surcharges to reflect the additional costs required.

Over the past five years tuitions have risen across the board, from 1-2 percent annually in some states, to an average of more than 5 percent—and well into the double figures for some private institutions. But this is not the fully story, for other related costs have also spiraled upwards dramatically. By 2002/03, many public colleges were projecting percentage increases in double figures. Some increases were stunning: 19 percent at the University of Iowa for in-state students; 21 percent at the University of North Carolina at Chapel Hill and 10 percent at Pennsylvania State University. Politicians and higher education officials continue to search for alternative methods of raising tuition, to avoid a public outcry against ever-higher tuitions.

The rising cost of public education, and the fear that it is financially squeezing some students out of a college education, has prompted some state universities to adopt a practice long used by private schools to attract students: tuition discounting. Colleges skim off some portion of tuition income, and use these dollars to pay for scholarships for those in more need. Those found funds can be substantial. Private schools do this routinely; typically some 40 percent of scholarship dollars is dispersed in tuition for the needy.

A stream of new, creative approaches to student tuitions and fees can be expected. The present rigid structures, wherein everyone pays the same tuition and which allow for in-state and out-of-state tuition, various scholarship and loan plans, will inevitably yield to greater use of discounts by students who commit early.

The consequences of tuition increases, even if they will dampen somewhat with time, could significantly limit access to higher education for many aspirants, particularly for the poor and the disadvantaged. This level of financial uncertainty is bad public policy and should not be acceptable. Indeed, there is already some danger of default on the nation's core commitment to equal access to higher education. The reason lies in the inability to manage public institutions as well as those in the private sector. The direct consequence of this trend is to deny access to those on the bottom rungs to America's dream of power through education. This is a serious issue of public policy and, to date, it has not been handled very well.

In their stewardship of public higher education, state governments try very hard to keep tuitions low for state residents, regardless of students' ability to pay, and to offer high-quality public education to all students. The University of California System has been experimenting with differential tuitions, geared to the specific incomes and wealth of families. However, it may be that such variable-rate plans could stretch middle-class families who have long enjoyed relatively low tuitions and fees. This approach gives the student the same feeling that airplane passengers have when they find that their seatmates only paid half the cost for the same seat that they paid, because they bought it earlier. With tight budgets and enrollments rising, state leaders are increasingly being forced to choose which of the three commitments above they can keep.[56]

Although the upward spiraling of tuitions and fees continues, public institutions are still seen as a real bargain. Yet there are many opportunities for further improvement. According to the College Board in 2002, annual tuition and fees for a four-year public college were about $3,800 for state residents, as compared to just over $17,000 for the average private college. Factoring in room and board, these figures

---

56. "As Tuitions Rise, What Will Happen to Quality and Access?" in *The Chronicle of Higher Education*, Sept. 19, 2003, pp. B7-B11.

average out to about $9,000 and $24,000, respectively. And according to Patrick Callan, Executive Director of the National Center for Public Policy and Higher Education, the irony of institutional budgeting is that the steepest tuition increases of the past 20 years have occurred during recessions, just when family incomes were declining or flat, and unemployment was up.

One approach to setting tuitions is the use of discounts on a sliding scale, based upon family income and resources. As just mentioned, experiments with various differential tuitions are helping students in college by paying what they realistically can afford. One version of this is the tiered plan, which charges incoming students more than returning ones. Over a period of four years the costs level out evenly, with all students down the line eventually paying about the same tuitions and fees in a given year. The University of Illinois is one institution that has done this successfully; some others are evaluating it. These plans offer guaranteed flat tuition plans for students throughout their four year class program. Another version is the so-called prepaid state college tuition plans. The premise here is that if families start investing in college accounts when their children are young, the money needed later for college will be in inflated, not current dollars. The glitch in this is that with ever-inflating tuitions, many families are simply not confident that this will turn out to be a good deal for them.

The fact is that any national solution to the tuition dilemma cannot hold tuitions at the same rate for all students. Rather, sufficient need-based aid has to be provided to prevent qualified students from being excluded from higher education simply for financial reasons. This dilemma is not new. In the early 1900s, all 4-year colleges had to increase tuitions and fees by as much as 24 percent a year, as America tried to dig itself out of the big recession. Hardest hit were the states of Massachusetts, Iowa, Missouri and Texas. Fully a third of all States labored under spending cuts of 10 percent or more. Ordinary students, trying to get their piece of the American Pie, found the emerging community college systems more affordable. The privileged, of course, have always had options. But at that time burgeoning costs, and little in the way of loans and scholarships, made it tough for average youths to prepare for professional careers.

What are the solutions? The prepaid state college tuition funding mechanism seems to be off to an uncertain start. More than a million US families are investing some $10 billion into these plans, with the expectation that if they pay tuition now, those same inflated dollars will take care of some of these costs in the future, when their children reach college age. Such programs have been around for years, but parents and students are increasingly having second thoughts about this way of gaining access to higher education.

When the economy is sturdy, there will always be new pressures to find better, more constructive ways to fund future students. State tuitions will climb that spiral ever and ever higher. Tuitions and fees at the Universities of California and Virginia shot up by some 30 percent in 2003; and by nearly 40 percent at the University of Arizona. Such policies can only hurt schools. Not surprisingly, the burden always falls most heavily on low income families.[57]

In fact, students have long been engaged in the practice of differential pricing, in the form of discounts such as loans and scholarships, and lab fees. A key feature of successfully implementing a variable-cost schedule is providing good information, and as early as possible. For transparency, students need to be given good and timely information that they can use to schedule their studies around the clock and around the year. They, as customers, should be entitled to have a range of dates, times and media that best fit into their particular calendars. Let them have the information, and entitle them to see how the various options play to their advantage or disadvantage, so that they can make informed decisions.[58]

College scholarships are yet another common path to pursuing higher education. Fully half of states offer academic scholarships for residents to study at their public universities. These scholarships are not

---

57. "Beyond their Reach," in the *U.S. News and World Report*, Sept. 8, 2003, pp. 50-54.
58. "Same Classroom, Different Price," in *The Chronicle of Higher Education*, Sept. 19, 2003, pp. A10-11.

only for top students. Indeed, many state scholarship programs can really help high school students who meet certain minimum academic standards. And the US government helps by providing some $70 billion to students in scholarships, loans and gifts.

Work-study programs and athletic scholarships are yet another important component for covering college expenses. They are essential for many students to be able to afford their college costs. They tend to be quite competitive. Alternatively, an increasing proportion of students must either stretch out the time to earn their degree, or go into a protected debt period extending well after graduation, or both. Some fortunate graduates will have their debts forgiven by their employers but, for most, the burden is theirs to manage.

Gaining popularity among families planning for their children's education are 529 Savings Plans.[59] Thanks to recent tax legislation, these state-sponsored college savings plans (known as "529 plans" after the section of the tax code that created them) are a very effective way for most people to save for college. The reason is simple: there are no Federal taxes. These funds are held and managed by states, not employers, and resemble Roth IRAs. Under the plan, families invest directly or through a broker, and the returns are tax free, as long as they are used for bona fide college expenses, such as room and board, and/or tuition.

Since 2001 the US government has allowed students to tap into the money they have accumulated in a 529 plan, tax free. This is a big departure from the past, when earnings were taxed at the student's income tax rate upon withdrawal. Several states have now waived their own taxes on these accounts, and more—though not all—are expected to follow. There is one hitch: the money must be used for higher education, or the student will have to pay taxes and a penalty, typically 10 percent of earnings.

Students need better access to new and affordable loans to enable them to pursue their educational goals. Most college students must borrow their tuition money from their own family, or from their college or university via the US Department of Education's direct loan plan.

---

59. "Give it The Old College Try with a 529 Plan," in *Business Week*, Sept. 24, 2001, p. 126.

However, colleges and universities do not always get the best deal that way, as mentioned earlier. These institutions often get lower interest rates by dealing through private lenders, such as Sallie Mae and state agencies which provide loans under a separate Federal plan. It is good for the university, for they assure a profit (by law, Uncle Sam is forbidden from such profiting). The trend toward private rather than Federal funding of tuitions may not be such a good deal for taxpayers, however, for they ultimately pay the check.

So, there are basically two main types of Federally-backed loans available. Students can borrow directly from the Federal government's plan, *or* they can borrow from a private lender. Many states are looking at Federal loan programs, and are replacing these traditional sources with private lenders and state agencies. Institutions like Michigan State University are making the switch, and are guaranteeing a net profit for the school, which the government is forbidden to do. At this time, more than 60 colleges and universities have terminated their relationships with the Education Department's direct loan program, and more are expected to follow.

Who or what is Sallie Mae? It is an effective, fully private, government-sponsored company that is entirely independent of the Federal Government. It is listed in both the Fortune 500 and Forbes 500 exchanges (www.salliemae.com), and is part of the Federal Family Education Loan Program, or FFEL. This agency gets its money from associate lender banks, such as Citibank and Bank One. Generally, colleges and universities subscribe to one, but not both approaches. The private lenders, of course, must bear all marketing costs, which often involves staffers who market to college administrators at various conferences and other venues. It is big business; as college tuitions and fees continue to increase, private lenders are eager providers. On average, graduates are leaving their alma maters with some $17,000 of debt.[60]

The Federal government got into the student grant business with the Pell Grants, first issued in 1972. They remain the government's principal means of providing aid for low-income students. A Pell Grant is a

---

60. "Big Money on Campus," in *The U.S. News & World Report*, Oct. 27, 2003, pp.30-40.

Federal grant for undergraduate students who do not already have a bachelor or professional degree. This grant can be augmented by other loans and other sources of support, as needed. The student is entitled to just one Pell Grant in an award year. The amount depends on factors such as cost of attendance, whether the student is a full-time or part-time student, and whether he or she will be attending for a full academic year. Some funds are available even for full-time students. Pell Grants typically do not cover the entire cost of attending a college or university, but it is a great enabler for those committed to pursuing a college education.

The fact is that colleges and universities have never really been accountable for cost control, and have had little incentive to be better and more efficient in the way they design their processes. There has been very little progress in the way that they deliver education; few innovations. They are, after all, classic oligopolies—a captive market with little real competition or innovation.

Attention will now turn to a subject that is vitally important to all educational institutions: measuring performance. Measurement is *most* important. As with any disciplined process, whether a college or a manufacturing line, people tend to measure and evaluate by what is easy and what looks good. Process experts say that, too often, what is easy to measure can often be misleading or just plain inappropriate. Authorities within academia are now beginning to understand this, and those who embrace this philosophy of measurement will be well rewarded. One of the author's personal missions is to coach educational leaderships about precisely how and why to use forward-looking processes to strengthen their institutions. There are literally hundreds of "point metrics" available for gauging actual organizational status. The challenge is to identify the minimal set of metrics that are necessary and sufficient to assess continually the organization's overall state of health. Not surprisingly, such easy-to-calculate factors as enrollments and faculty salaries are the least useful.

Schools must become more entrepreneurial in the face of ever-rising costs, by focusing upon new sources of revenues, and by shedding waste and inefficiency. They need to become more creative in finding new opportunities from such operations as university bookstores and dining halls, parking lots, copy and other service centers and a wide assortment of others. Given these mounting challenges, it is not surprising that institutional fundraising today is big business. It is even more imperative in the face of increasing competition from the for-profit educational sector.

One simple approach to finding process efficiencies is to make an institution's assets (classrooms, auditoriums and labs, for instance) better utilized. In particular, there is a need to rethink the approach to scheduling courses. Most of the above assets are used less than ten percent of the time in a 24-hour day, 7-day week; even less if one considers the near emptiness of these assets during the summer months. For example, certain classes might be designated for discounted tuitions, for courses that can be scheduled at odd times such as evenings or weekends. This would make for better use of facilities, and in time there would be cost benefits. Renting and leasing space to companies for the purpose of corporate training and development can be mutually beneficial. Such schemes would appeal generally to working adults, and students who may favor nontraditional times and days for their lectures and lab sessions. As a result, the schemes could actually lead to incremental increases in student numbers.

There are also financial benefits for institutions in engaging in group purchasing, allowing them to buy commodities ranging from dormitory mattresses and paper goods to computers and other necessities at quantity discounts. These agreements can be competitive, and suppliers are selected on the basis of price, quality, capability and service offered.

Ultimately, the institutions themselves must manage their budgets much better, through becoming more efficient in their operations. The first step is to have specific, measurable plans that draw the line on expenses, and then find ways to be more creative with customer service. It will mean doing things differently. The new pathways that will be needed for traditional and professional people of all ages must be accepted and embraced. As mentioned in Chapter 3, the traditional education formula (high school, four years in college, and then a career) may be the legacy, but it is certainly not the future.

Chapter V: The New Business of Higher Education

Trends to Watch

The vast majority of American college students today are educated at public institutions.[61] The US pioneered the concept that higher education should be available to all its citizens, and particularly so in the post-World War II era. College programs were opened to people of all races, creeds and nationalities. Federal and state coffers opened to create new and expanded campuses that multiplied tenfold the pre-war academic infrastructure.

Public community colleges and universities then enrolled some 80 percent of college men and women. They struggled to offer programs that students needed, and were vulnerable to the forces of population demographics and the high expectations of better futures. Schools are now beginning to reap the economic benefit of a better understanding of the way they operate, such as from using more contract services, buying smarter, and more efficient utilization of existing facilities. Also, financial aid coffers are draining, just when the needs for financial assistance are soaring. As a benchmark, more than 80 percent of undergraduate students receive some kind of financial aid. Clearly, part of the solution should lie in the appropriate use of educational technologies that have the promise of delivering course content better, and cheaper.

A few colleges and universities have begun to downsize their faculties, even as enrollments are still growing. They simply need to be more efficient. Of the approximately one million faculty members in the United States, some 200,000 are full-time adjuncts. Universities employ about 15 percent fewer tenured professors that they did in 1985. All faculties are zealous in protecting their rights regarding traditional continuing tenure. The great academic institutions need to invest more in technologies that will create efficiencies and better learning. And they need to recruit and train a new cadre of faculty members, and equip them in their use.

Professor Donald Heller at Pennsylvania State University's Center for the Study of Higher Education acknowledges that[62], indeed, non-

---

61. "Colleges in Crisis," in *Business Week*, April 28, 2003, pp. 73-79.

profit colleges must meet many standards that for-profit businesses do not. Higher education boards in most states subject their public institutions to reporting regulations that go above and beyond the minimal reporting required of all licensed post-secondary institutions. For example, public institutions are often required to submit program plans to boards, and to report annual progress toward meeting key goals at a level of detail that proprietary, for-profit institutions do not generally do. In addition, the financial statements of public colleges are readily available to legislative panels, Executive Branch agencies and individual citizens. News-media representatives can easily secure state and institutional audit reports which disclose significant information about the inner workings of public institutions. Student newspapers regularly publish the salaries of each faculty member and administrator. Freedom of Information laws in many states allow wide access to facts about various aspects of public colleges, including salaries, presidential searches, and institutional compliance with Federal, state and local laws. For-profit institutions are not obliged to publish this kind of information.

Anyone interested in obtaining financial information about private nonprofit colleges can usually find it in the IRS 990 forms. Most of the information is available via web sites such as guidestar.com, an online clearinghouse of information about nonprofit organizations. Their reports include the salaries and benefits of the top officers of each college, as well as detailed statements on the institution's revenues, expenses, assets, and liabilities.

The good news is that many of the new for-profits are doing something particularly well: making money.[63] Private equity funds are an increasingly prominent investment option for some of the largest college endowments. And the trend has spawned a curious side effect: some traditional colleges are becoming significant, if passive, investors in for-

---

62. "Not All Institutions are Alike," by Donald E. Heller, in *The Chronicle of Higher Education*, Nov. 14, 2003, pp. B7-B8.
63. "For-Profit Colleges Attract a Gold Rush of Investors," in *The Chronicle of Higher Education*, March 14, 2003, pp. A25-26.

profit education. Brown University, Dartmouth College, the Johns Hopkins University, and Washington University of St. Louis are all investors in various private equity funds that are buying up for-profit college companies. Harvard University invests in at least two such funds. Institutions that are being acquired are privately held, so most of this action—which is serving to strengthen for-profit colleges and further consolidate the career-college industry—is taking place below the radar of policy makers and higher education leaders. Private equity is not a new phenomenon in the industry. Before going public, several of the companies that are the darlings of Wall Street, including Career Education and Corinthian, began their growth with private equity backing.

Faculty and Staff

For too long, institutions of higher learning have built upon two factions—faculty and administration. This schism has hampered them from engaging in the work of teaching and research for the betterment of students. There has always been some friction between these cultures. Moreover, this breeds a suboptimal behavior that steals energy and trust throughout the institution. There will always be differences of opinion and process, but as has been mentioned, a true team will accommodate specific compromises for the greater good of long-term excellence. Therefore, the work of the trustees and senior officers of the institution is to *lead*. Difficult decisions must be made, and they inevitability will disappoint some. But in the long term, effective leadership will flatten out the bumps on the road, and make the future better for everyone.

It is not in the culture of shared governance to encourage academics to seek out ways to deliver better education at less cost. Tenure and modest salary increases are regarded as entitlements of these institutions, even when not justified by continual improvements. Efforts to beat back cost escalations have generally been focused simply on increasing class sizes. And faculty salaries tend to languish at increases well below those in government or the private sector. For presidents, the mantra is, "The good news is that enrollment is up; the bad news is that the enrollment is up." Academics worry about it, but have not yet found the levers needed to tune up their enterprise. Some examples are given below.[64]

- Cap enrollments by imposing tougher admission standards
- Replace regular faculty with adjuncts (or term appointments)
- Increase tuitions and fees
- Seek new, more powerful and more efficient ways to educate students
- Trim administrative costs via outsourcing and other mechanisms
- Use information technologies to their highest productive levels
- Seek new, additional sources of revenue

Salaries for university presidents, especially those in public institutions, continue to move up and are with presidents of private schools. The days when public university presidents earned far less than their peers at top private institutions are waning and private donations are playing a greater role to help make up the differences. Many presidents and chancellors in the public sector now get supplemental packages from private sources. This development is, in part, occasioned by the fact that fewer and fewer qualified people choose to take the top jobs, because of the stress and obligations involved. Therefore, compensations at some public schools are rising toward $750K and over.

One new area of concern comes from the growing gender disparity among college-educated men and women.[65]

Table 5.1. Breakdown of Salaries by Gender

	Men	Women	(Women's Salaries less than Men's by x) (in percent)
Bachelor's Degree	$62,543	$40,263	36%
Master's Degree	$75,441	$49,635	34%
Prof. Degree (MD, LLB)	$130,711	$72,171	45%
PhD	$107,988	$69,085	36%

These gender data tend to be somewhat skewed in that men, on average, have more years experience in these categories than women. And there is still a lot of subtle, unconscious discrimination in hiring decisions.

---

64. "Budget Cuts Force Community Colleges to Consider Turning Away Students," in *The Chronicle of Higher Education*, July 26, 2002, pp. A25-26.
65. The *Chicago Sun Times*, April 10, 2001, p. 2.

Moreover, there is a new trend: the migration of faculty from public to private institutions. More faculty members than ever are launching their careers in public institutions, then, when they have established themselves as scholars, teachers and researchers, they seek positions in private institutions where the economic rewards are better. Up until the 1980s, salaries among public and private faculty were about at parity. This is no longer the case, and the beneficiaries are those at private colleges and universities. The gaps are significant. In the 80s private institutions compensated their faculties by about $1,300 more per year than their state-supported colleagues. But by 1997-98, this differential had jumped to $21,700 per faculty member. The reason for this is that private institutions have been far more aggressive and successful in developing their endowments. Most of these institutions have been much better in getting their alums to endow professorships, scholarships and buildings.

Public institutions are rightfully concerned and are stepping up efforts to get their wealthy graduates to contribute more. But it is a hard sell. Furthermore, these same schools are being squeezed as legislators expect them to raise more funds and curtail their reliance on state subsidies. Among major state institutions, capital campaigns exceeding $1 billion are not unusual. In keeping with these trends, more top level high school graduates are opting for private colleges, simply because these schools can provide more tuition relief than public schools. The only answer is for the public institutions to become much better at delivering education, at fundraising, and to be more effective in running their institutions.

Americans need to pay much more attention to making their colleges and universities more productive and efficient. That can be achieved without losing quality. A perfect example can be found in tiny Hillsdale College, west of Detroit in Michigan, which has just 1,200 students. President George Roche has held that office for 28 years—four times the average tenure for presidents. Hillsdale refuses to take any Federal dollars, not even for Federally-backed loans. Its tuition is $13,000 for students who do not have scholarships. In 1998 it took in $80 million and spent just $35 million on operations. Roche has built up the endowment over the years from $4 million to nearly $200 million, and annual investment returns provide over $40 million for operations. Graduates and other friends of Hillsdale give to the tune of 24 percent of its endowment—compared to about just 4 percent for most colleges. Those dollars provide twice the amount needed annually for the academic budget. Moreover, rather that raising large endowments for the college to lend money to students, Hillsdale pledges their endowment as collateral for loans from banks, and lends the proceeds to students at prevailing rates. Faculty members earn modest salaries, and teach four courses a semester (the national average is three). However, these teachers only teach; there is no pressure or expectation for research, grantsmanship or publication of scholarly articles.

What are the implications of these new pressures of change? . Smaller public colleges will struggle to keep admissions affordable at traditional levels. State legislatures are finding it ever harder to fund them adequately. The new pitch-word of public higher education is the transition from the state *supported* school, to state *assisted*, and inevitably, to the state *located* school. Although state institutions continue now to be the main source of funding of higher education across the nation, their share continues to shrink. This trend further shifts the educational burden from taxpayers to corporations and wealthy alums.

Another point to be considered is that the US simply has too many traditional colleges and universities; 3,600—more than any other nation in the world. There are too many for the overall system to be truly efficient. Most are not practiced or polished in pursing their missions, as becomes clear when they are measured against other categories of public and private institutions.

In his book[66] Cornell University Professor Ronald Ehrenbert makes the point again that US colleges and universities are essentially locked into a pattern of ever-rising costs. The reasons: endowment policies, admissions and financial aid policies, and a lack of programs financed at a level adequate to meet the needs of the growing number of low-income students. Add to this an ever-growing research infrastructure, inefficient

---

66. "Tuition Rising," in *The Chronicle of Higher Education*, April 18, 2003, p. B20.

library collections, intercollegiate athletics, tenure and the lifting of mandatory retirement for faculty, and there are all the ingredients of bad business.

Ehrenbert points to some of the basic deficiencies of colleges and universities: loose budget constraints, weak authority lines, state political vulnerabilities, inefficient institutional designs, and faculties stuck in a mire of sameness. Tuitions at the larger public institutions have risen over the past few years at an annual rate of about four percent, to cover the costs of continuing inefficiencies. Some of those incremental costs go to increasing administrative overheads, often reaching levels of 3–4 administrative staff for each professor/instructor. It is hardly surprising to find that it is rare for a president to achieve consensus and take needed systemic approaches to leveling out costs. Furthermore, teaching and learning is a labor-intensive enterprise, and therefore has limits as to efficiency and economies of scale, unlike the industrial sector. Given this, there is a duty to see how effective and efficient it can be.

In recent years administrators have faced questions of sexual harassment, tenure battles, athletic payoffs and other important but distracting issues on campus. Below are some practical measures for preventing legal entanglements which commonly face administrators:[67]

- Have senior administrators make arrangements for getting effective legal advice: not abnegation, nor embattlement, just simple good sense.
- Encourage campus leaders to cooperate with one another in preventive planning; get your lawyers and administrators to talk to each other, frequently, and expose each group to seminars, etc., on the other side's function. Each must be bilingual in their understanding.
- Train your compliance officers to identify early warning signs of legal problems.
- Perform regular audits of the legal health of the institution and identify areas of significant risk.
- Develop programs and agendas which will engage institutional leaders in areas of ethical, pedagogical, administrative, financial, and mission-driven effort.
- Engage institutional leaders in a continuing program of legal planning.

---

67. "Preventive Law: How Colleges Can Avoid Legal Problems," in *The Chronicle of Higher Education*, April 18, 2003, p. B20.

- Establish internal grievance, mediation, and other dispute resolution mechanisms to help forestall formal legal action.

4. Tenure and Collective Bargaining

Like many academics, this author has a problem with tenure and the stranglehold it continues to have on collegiate institutions. A pivotal experience back in the early 1980s shaped my attitudes on this issue, when I was a professor and department chair at the Illinois Institute of Technology. At that time, this was the largest department in the university, and was certainly one of the best of its kind anywhere. It had great students and a strong faculty, many with international reputations. But there was one member there who was an anchor around the necks of the students, staff and faculty. Once a leading figure in his field, he had allowed his performance to deteriorate and he had developed a less than constructive attitude. He would berate students and humiliate them publicly; and he consistently posted by far the lowest student evaluations. For years he had failed to do any research or writing, and had not worked in the field for some time; nor had he kept pace with changes in teaching methodology.

Being new to the position and a little naïve, I took it as a special challenge to get this man back on track. I tried every approach imaginable. I offered help and incentives; smaller classes and more attractive schedules; his own computer and help in using it. Other faculty members who had known the professor much longer were consulted and their advice sought. As the months passed, it became clear that he was not going to make any real effort to improve and that, in fact, he was just playing mind games. The time came for action.

I talked to his dean, and then with all his faculty colleagues about retiring their colleague (he was over 60 years of age). Without exception, each agreed and said it was time for action. In accordance with written academic procedure, a secret ballot of the department's tenured faculty was held. The vote for him to be retired was unanimous. Some weeks later, a similar vote was taken by all among the tenured faculty in the

College of Engineering. There was the same unanimous result. Finally, the case was put to the entire faculty of the university. The faculty voted *not* to have the professor retired, and that he should be permitted to carry on as before, without correction or reprimand.

The faculty's position was that, while the gentleman in question was, indeed, a very poor performer and had an unacceptable attitude, they simply could not break tenure. They were concerned that it would set a precedent which might make it easier in the future to have others removed. One member of the department said, in effect, that the cost of breaking tenure was just too high. "Who's next?" he asked.

For the author, this was a defining moment. All the noble rhetoric about academic truth and purity counted for nothing. Deep convictions are apparently no match for a threat to the collective brotherhood.

This kind of incident is rare, but every institution has its own version. The larger issue is how an institution should deal appropriately with a wayward professor. Resolving the issue to everyone's satisfaction is difficult, but it must be faced. In this particular situation, the author worked with the individual and with other faculty members to coach and encourage him to recover from his recent lapses. And, to some extent, it worked.

Traditionally, tenure—or continuous tenure, as it is properly known—is an appointment that continues within one institution until retirement. It is valuable in that faculty members who have achieved tenure generally are allowed more latitude in their research, teaching and outside affairs. Generally, non-tenured faculty do not have a contractual right to tenure.

Tenure has long been a pillar of the academic profession. It is honored and spoken of as a right for those who have earned it. However, most believe that tenure is as much a duty as right, and that any right carries corresponding responsibilities. These rights include performing well in teaching, scholarship and institutional service duties. But, as with any human process, it can break down, requiring care and attention to repair when needed.

As generally understood, tenure is an institutional process that attempts to bring stability and rewards to faculty. It is distinct from other employment arrangements, where tenure is only granted for finite terms such as five-year intervals. Tenure is a process whose purpose is to give selected faculty members indefinite and secure appointments until retirement, or until separated from the institution.

Most people argue in favor of having faculty that are, in a sense, fire-proofed. Scholars should and must have independence in their pursuit of teaching and in their long-term intellectual pursuits. Tenure is the principal tool that institutions have to reward top scholars and teachers who are, in their respective fields, regarded as among the finest in the world. But tenure is now being used in a wider context, taking on a different, blurred meaning from the original, as defined above. And it is precisely this blurring that causes problems, and ignites heated debate on the subject. Each institution has its own clearly written policies which set out the standards to be met. And, of course, politics can and often does become a factor in the success (or failure) of a candidate's petition for tenure.

Tenure processes include legal employment contracts. Deans and department heads use these to set goals which encompass teaching, research and service. There are many new variations of this basic tenure employment contract. They may provide for such terms as severability (for appropriate cause or continuing delinquency of service) and duration (five years, for instance). Other features can be built in, as appropriate. Tenure can differ in many minor details among institutions.

Any tenure process should be transparent, have accountabilities, and be fair. Occasionally, however, there can be problems with particular contractual elements which, in turn, invite challenges. Individual faculty members who are denied tenure must always have avenues of grievance and redress, as spelled out in the institution's written rules, policies and regulations. These individuals have full rights of appeal to the institution's president or chancellor, and even to the civil and Supreme Court systems. The procedures must be clear. Administrators are obligated to maintain a fair and thorough evaluation of all faculty candidates, in accordance with the written policies of the particular institution. These issues can get sticky, however, for the courts have only limited authority in areas of institutional policy, which can lead to frustration.

Climbing the ladder to tenure within highly competitive institutions is notoriously difficult. The details of the tenure process, as indicated, vary with each particular institution. Some have formal track procedures (teaching position leading to tenure); others do not.

One group of universities which tends to set the pace for others regarding tenure is the Ivy League. The tenure processes within the League vary widely. A short summary of the practice of each college is given below:

Brown has a formal tenure track; professors come up in their sixth year for consideration. No plans to review its process.

Columbia has no formal tenure track. Untenured professors must achieve tenure within eight years or leave. Under review.

Cornell has a formal tenure track; faculty members generally come up in their sixth year for consideration. No plans for a formal review.

Dartmouth has a formal tenure track; assistant professors serve a three year appointment and most, but not all, get reappointed for another three years and then come up for tenure at the end of their sixth year.

Harvard has no formal tenure track; untenured professors in the faculty of arts and sciences can stay as long as eight years before they must leave. The faculty is now reforming its tenure process.

University of Pennsylvania (Penn) has a formal tenure track, generally six years long. Under review.

Princeton has a formal tenure track; junior professors typically come up for review in their sixth year. Planning to review their process.

Yale has no formal tenure track; untenured professors can stay as long as ten years before they must leave. Under review.

Tenure is being challenged and assaulted more than ever before, and is slowly being watered down. Former British Prime Minister Margaret Thatcher, herself once an academic, began in the 1980s to phase out tenure in Britain's higher education system. Soon after, the Carnegie Foundation for the Advancement of Teaching provided another benchmark. In 1989 this organization carried out an audit which revealed that 20 percent of all faculty, 32 percent of women faculty, and 39 percent of faculty under 39 years of age, agreed that "abolition of tenure would, on the whole, improve the quality of American higher education." A more recent survey by the Higher Education Research Institute at UCLA found that 39 percent of faculty agreed that "tenure is an outmoded concept." There is clearly an increasing momentum toward modifying this practice, or abolishing it altogether.

And this tenure debate is not confined to academics. The American Association for Higher Education (AAHE) has concluded that there are advantages to "other pathways"—i.e. outside of tenure—for careers in colleges and universities. In particular, the AAHE has found that the growing number of part-time and non-tenure-track faculty members in the professoriate are "satisfied" with their status, that younger aspirants for tenure would be glad to have it eliminated, and that institutional flexibility can survive only in a free market employment environment. Moreover, the crest of the Baby Boom wave will soon have passed, and there will be fewer students on campuses.

There are differing levels of interest in the issue of tenure. A study by Harvard University in 2000 showed that 48 percent of private institutions have, and use, some kind of tenure review policy. These policies vary from "soft" (here are some tools, please try them to improve upon your weaknesses), to "hard" (levy mandatory sanctions for faculty getting poor reviews, up to and including forfeiting their tenure privilege).

In 1996 the president of the NASULGC (National Association of State Universities and Land-Grant Colleges) was on record as saying that "academia risks becoming an Edsel if it does not more searchingly question tenure." It creates large inequities among faculty who, ostensibly, have about the same duties and responsibilities. And well-known educational attorney Ronald B. Standler says that it is established law that untenured professors are mere employees "with the same legal right as a waitress in a restaurant or a clerk in a store." He argues further that academic freedom does not apply to teachers in elementary and high schools, because:

- School teachers teach well-known facts and methods.
- School teachers rarely write scholarly works.
- School teachers have pupils that are between 5 and 18 years of age.
- School teachers usually have only a bachelor's or master's degree with a major subject of "education."
- School teachers use textbooks that are chosen by state educational committees.
- School teachers are required to follow a standard syllabus.

In short, Standler says that teachers are not always academics.

In a move that the American Association of University Professors (AAUP) called "a historic breakthrough," a group of full-time adjunct faculty members at Western Michigan University won the right in 2003 to become eligible for tenure. Others, including the University of Cincinnati and Emerson University, are also chalking up successes in organizing their part-time faculty. They are called academic career specialists, or faculty specialists. These educators have continuing tenure and can only be fired for cause or due to financial exigencies. They do not have to conduct scholarly research in order to earn tenure.

Table 5.2 Changing Tenure Policies: Western Michigan University

	Old System	New System
Faculty Status	Not part of the faculty	Part of faculty
Salary Minimums	Equal to those or regular Faculty members (except for language specialists Have no salary minimums)	Same
Contracts	1-yr renewable, fiscal-year-renewable, or continuing	Eligible for tenure
Tenure	Not possible	Possible
Evaluations	Based on teaching, licensing or skills, and service	Same
Termination	Mid-contract firing possible only for cause or financial exigency	Same
Layoffs	Possible if position is no longer needed or $ is not available	Same
Workload	24 credit hours/year, like That of regular faculty members	30 credit hours

This highlights another trend among colleges and universities. There is an increasing proportion of full-time faculty members who are not eligible for tenure. Opponents fear that this trend will lead to hiring adjuncts without appropriate advanced degrees. Indeed, a key issue in many of these struggles is the specific focus on part-time faculty. Of the approximate one million faculty members in the United States, some 200,000 today are full-time adjunct members.[68]

In a letter to the editor by R. Luke Evans, Special Projects Coordinator, New England Complex Systems Institute, Cambridge, Massachusetts, published in *The Chronicle of Higher Education*,[69] he said,

> While the difference at Western MI University may be beneficial to certain individuals from a job-security standpoint, I wonder what it may mean for the university down the road, as it adapts to changing student and community needs. My views on tenure are quite conservative—and perhaps unrealistic. I believe that to be eligible for tenure, one should hold a terminal degree. Special categories of instruction without terminal degrees should be eligible for renewable contracts of varying lengths. Only full professors should be eligible for tenure. Lower-rank professors should have contractual arrangements similar to this for instructors. Five-year contracts may provide more job security for excellent instructors and associate professors without undue insecurity if one is performing well, and would still provide the institution with the flexibility it needs. Reviews would occur during the fourth year and, if necessary, the instructor could begin making plans to move elsewhere. Of course, unions would be necessary to help assure fairness. Tenure should be reserved for those who have demonstrated that they are at the top of their respective fields in teaching, research and community service.

In yet another recent realignment, the University of Michigan at Ann Arbor has made a pact with its professors and lecturers who are not on a tenure track, to create a union to represent their some 1,300 full- and part-time professors. Representing this group is the Lecturers' Employee Organization, an affiliate of the American Federation of Teachers.

Another interesting trend is that larger institutions are looking outside for administrative services.[70] In some campuses, part-time professors teach more than half of the classes. Part-time faculty can have different ranks, depending on their experience. Some private schools have unionized, including Emerson College (Boston) and New York Uni-

---

68. "Widening the Tenure Track," in *The Chronicle of Higher Education*, January 3, 2003, pp. A8-12. "Some Adjuncts at Western Michigan University Win Right to Tenure," in *The Chronicle of Higher Education*, November 15, 2003, p. A15.
69. "Letter to the editor" by R. Luke Evans, Special Projects Coordinator, New England Complex Systems Institute, Cambridge, MA: in *The Chronicle of Higher Education*, Feb. 7, 2003, p. B4
70. "United We Stand," in *The Chronicle of Higher Education*, Feb. 21, 2003.

versity. The main issues are pay and benefits, including health benefits, equal parking privileges, and more job security. Part-time teaching agreements are now lasting beyond age 70, and are seen as necessary and appropriate. Status is important to tenured faculty, something they do not want to share. They see it as threat number one; college administrators see it from a very different perspective.

Florida Gulf Coast University (Fort Myers, Florida), which opened in 1997, now offers tenure only in a few exceptional circumstances. Their policy is to replace tenure with 3-5 year contracts, with the expectation that most professors' contracts will automatically rollover. Interestingly enough, despite their no-tenure policy, some faculty have decided to leave upon finding tenure-track positions elsewhere.

Mitchell College, a small, two-year college in New London, Connecticut, was forced by escalating cost and declining enrollments to abandon continuous tenure.[71] Its faculty members are now given one-year contracts, with the expectation that their employment will continue. Mitchell had to make the layoffs because the student body had declined to under 400 students, and it was losing money. Around 20 other institutions over the past three decades have had to do the same. Mitchell is in better shape than before because of this action. Enrollment is up, and the budget has been balanced since the actions.

In a related movement, union leaders are zealous in their efforts to organize graduate students and create collective bargaining units. More than 30 schools in America have them already. Organizers also see these students as employees of the institution, when they are paid teaching and research assistants. Dissenters contend that these men and women are exploited, merely temporary employees and, therefore, simply do not have the authority to unionize. It is a tough, ongoing fight, in large part because of the rapid and continual student turnover.

In July, 2004 everything was overturned when the National Labor Relations Board ruled that graduate students at private colleges and uni-

---

71. "A College Drops Tenure to Stay Alive," in *The Chronicle of Higher Education*, April 26, 2002, pp. A12-14.

versities do not have the right to form unions. Schools, including Brown University and New York University had, since the year 2000, given graduate students the right to unionize. But that right was rescinded with the ruling. Unions held, and were supported by the decision, that the imposition of collective bargaining on graduate students would improperly intrude into the educational process. They maintained that graduate student assistants are primarily students and have only an educational, not economic, relationship with their institution. Some speculators are waiting to see whether this ruling might influence other private institutions under this same philosophy.

A new era has arrived. The National Labor Relations Board had ruled in 2000, that teaching assistants (TAs) at New York University could unionize under Federal labor law. Several universities accordingly have held elections to do just that. This is going to be a prolonged and arduous struggle for academia. College administrators hold that TAs are students, and not employees of the institution. Some lawyers for TAs have viewed them differently, as paid temporary employees of the college or university at which they work.

Educational administrators, of course, favor employee contracts rather than continuing tenure because it affords them flexibility, as well as economy, in fulfilling their teaching mission. Tenure is now evolving from a strict right to an institutional objective, but with some particular new elements. Some institutions are granting tenure to associate professors also, but not continual.

Northwestern University has a modern and fair approach to liberating traditional tenure contracts. They offer five-year-term contracts to some of their regular faculty, including those in their esteemed McCormick School of Engineering. The intention is that these faculty members will continue to teach and pursue their research interests until retirement. However, these agreements specifically contain an escape clause, for those few teachers who, for whatever reasons, do not perform well under acceptable standards, as measured by student and faculty surveys.

The Rochester Institute of Technology (RIT) started, back in the mid-nineties, to look for a way to "salvage" tenured faculty who were no longer doing their fair share in terms of teaching, research, advising, and stewardship. Historically, continuous tenure had been an entitlement that once won, was not dependent upon the professor's ability to live up to his or her obligation to the institution. RIT's president, Albert Simone, sought an acceptable way to untie the Gordian knot of enthusing again those who were letting down the Institute, yet severing those who were taking advantage of the tenure privilege and not improving. He was able to do this by marshalling his faculty and administrative staff to find a workable compromise. Simone created a committee of faculty and administrators to develop policy recommendations. The approach focused upon recharging fallen faculty members and having an annual review policy. It provided various approaches, tailored to the needs of the individual, to help them become more productive, fulfilled and contributive member of the faculty. While the emphasis was on helping the failing faculty members, termination was the inevitable result if they did not take the chance to improve their performance. It is the obligation of all RIT faculty members to keep up to date in their fields, teach effectively, and generally add appropriate value to their department and to the institution itself. The small sector of seriously underperforming faculty is estimated at less than ten percent.

In some cases, tenure can become a luxury the institution can no longer afford. An example comes from small Bennington College in Vermont. This prestigious four-year liberal arts college recently took the bold step of eliminating tenure altogether. President Elizabeth Coleman had the agonizing job of axing a third of the faculty members, and did away with tenure for those who remained. One faculty member philosophized, "Business people don't have tenure, why do academics need it?"

Of course, on occasion a tenured professor will abrogate, or even take advantage of, his/her contract by failing to meet the reasonable expectations of the institution. This might take the form of poor teaching, ethical matters or other shortcomings, and is sometimes a result of burnout. But these circumstances are uncommon, and are best handled administratively.

A variation on the Bennington College theme can be found at Olin College of Engineering, established in Needham, Massachusetts in 1999. Olin has no tenured positions at all. Rather, it seeks out the very best faculty it can find, and pays them what they require (as in the free market). According to Lawrence Milas, Chairman of the F.W. Olin Foundation which funds and operates the college, another important element of Olin's culture is its commitment to free tuition. Milas says that "Every time you increase tuition, you create a greater need for financial aid." He likens tuition to a house of cards, ultimately liable to collapse of its own weight. He might be right, but few institutions are sufficiently endowed to do what Olin is doing.

Some will say that higher education without tenure might create, in time, a system of training schools whose instructors would be neither educators nor scholars. But others strongly disagree with these extreme fears. Still, colleges and universities have generally not yet stepped up to the plate, as they should, with better alternatives that are in harmony with changing times. They need to offer sensible approaches that will keep the best of the tenure system, while creating trigger points for those few faculty members who are not meeting their own commitment to the spirit of continuous tenure. Indeed, this is precisely why there is a burgeoning adjunct faculty category, with a mechanism to hire and fire at will.

This certainly means that there will be a much greater variety of careers, necessitating lifelong learning. Colleges and universities will have to seize the opportunity and play a much stronger role in adult and continuing education. Colleges and universities will need seriously to transform their missions and cultures to compete effectively in this new era of opportunity.

Efficiency—a term seldom used in the context of higher education—will be more essential than ever in the new order. There are already larger fractions of faculties that have adjunct or term appointments (typically three to five years) which may or may not be renewed.

Tenured faculty will continue to be a significant element in the makeup of colleges and universities—but it will gradually become less common. For one thing, tenure appointments represent a significant fixed cost to the institution. In the language of American commerce, an institution has an obligation to shareholders (state and federal governments, donors and families) to be as efficient with its invested capital as possible. Every underused asset, including a poorly performing faculty, should either be repaired, or retired.

There is no doubt but that college administrators have increasingly relied upon part-timers and adjuncts to carry the instructional mission, perhaps overly so. Nearly half of all courses today are being delivered by non-tenured-track teaching staff. These teachers are paid less, sometimes substantially less, than regular faculty members. These soldiers of fortune have no real assurance of continuing service, and serve at the pleasure of their administration.

Such innovations are reasonable, appropriate and vital to the collective higher institution mission. The majority of faculty members have the determination to continue performing at their peak level well after gaining tenure. Some, of course, will regress and coast along. Any institution has its fraction of faculty that will lose its edge or competency to teach and inspire students. But this also represents a significant drain on the institution. Administrations are increasingly aware of these risks and will continue to find appropriate means to cope with them. On the other hand, all institutions have an obligation to offer counsel and to retrain any faculty member that seems to be losing his or her competency, with appropriate tools and understanding.

One of the most important challenges faced today in higher education is how best to integrate and coordinate various functions across the entire institution. The focus, strategically, should be on new processes and policies that are vital to better futures. As stated before, colleges and universities must do a much better job of inventing new ways to collaborate that will shed traditional inefficiencies, such as bureaucratic departments and inefficient schools, offices, and laboratories. This extends to administrators and, indeed, all the way up to trustees and governing boards. These leaders have much to give in terms of experience and institutional development. Most are strongly represented by industrial executives, and can be even more helpful in creating lines of leadership—if their counsel is solicited. It will be a tough, ongoing fight, but the mission of leadership is vital to improvement for the institution as a whole, not just its parts.

This period marks the first in modern times wherein tenure is being challenged as a prerequisite within academia. The debate is likely to continue for some time. Apologists in favor of traditional tenure systems argue that, increasingly, diminished protections will destroy the very foundation of professional and academic integrity. Many disagree.

5. THE WORKFORCE OF THE FUTURE: KNOWLEDGE

This chapter concludes with a glimpse at what lies ahead for higher education. It is accepted that scholars will have very different professional lives. The era of lifelong learning is beginning. In line with the surge of knowledge workers in the years ahead, there will ever-tighter alliances between industry and academia. Those institutions will be successful which provide such workers in the workplace with relevant skill-building programs. They will make deals with the private sector to outsource for education and training needs. With the explosion of online, video, multimedia conferencing and self-paced courses now offered by the private sector, in-house training sessions will become less cost-effective and convenient to use.

In addition to falling demographics, more people will migrate from traditional labor practices, and will become knowledge workers. This was discussed in Chapter II, Section 4. A significant implication of this is that people will continue to be productively employed well beyond the current limits. Add to this the medical advances which will keep people healthier for longer, and it can be anticipated that fewer workers will work over longer spans of years. As the demand for knowledge workers increases in comparison to the supply, corporations will offer to pay for education in return for future work.

Colleges and workers may use short courses and seminars, online content and distance learning for mutual benefit. This will be enormously important as people try to be everywhere at once. There will also be more use of cross appointments in which a knowledge worker can split his/her responsibilities between the school and the workplace. These linkages between industry and academia will create their own dynamics and tensions. As academics and public/private leaders become more closely engaged, some academic freedoms will likely fall away. Industrialists will expect to have some influence over curricula and pedagogy, in return for the funding they provide. And students, who traditionally have had no say in what or how faculty teaches, will have a voice.

Knowledge workers will replace institutional capital with their own personal intellectual capital in their workplaces, real and virtual. Work will be done at the office and at the plant, at home and around the world. Workers will be in high demand because of inadequate human supplies. And with a growing dependence on knowledge workers, it will be the workers that will own the means of production, not the employers—a profoundly different ballgame. Moreover, knowledge workers will acquire more and better portable skills because of the emphasis on continually honing knowledge and skills. People will work longer, and for a greater number and variety of organizations. As a consequence of these various factors, the tendency will be to have more careers and more employers.

This will certainly necessitate lifelong learning. Colleges and universities clearly will have to play a much stronger role in adult and continuing education. This new era will require the adoption of new technologies, missions and cultures in order to compete effectively.

This will become an era of activism. Even today, every aspect of the academic institution is being inspected to ensure that the fundamental issues of access, collective bargaining, fairness and excellence will be available for all. This is good, for institutional leaderships will need to lead and become more engaged. And academic leaders will need to accommodate these changes to serve the needs of working and older students.

In conclusion, a reminder of the very basis of this book: that accelerating social change will drive higher education in the years ahead, and that it is already beginning to touch everyone. Many will fear, or simply ignore, the changes ahead; it is certainly unsettling. But they must be open to the challenges, for there is no alternative. The great automobile magnate Charles Kettering said that, although the world hates change, it is the only thing that has brought progress.

Chapter VI: Getting the Most, While Managing Costs

Topical Themes
1. Teaching and Learning: Are Students Getting What They Need?
2. College Athletics and Recreation
3. Measuring Educational Outcomes
4. Learning by Degrees

1. Teaching and Learning: Are Students Getting What They Need?

It is time for a bold reconstruction of academic institutions. Throughout this book the pace of change and the needs of colleges and universities have been highlighted. The list is long; this is what lies ahead:

- Reining in education costs
- Creating new teaching approaches and tools
- Finding ways to become more effective and efficient, and to relax dependency upon tenure
- Impending downturn in the US population
- Growth in knowledge workers
- People having more careers
- Steady rise of for-profit colleges and universities
- Flexible work arrangements
- Lifelong learning

Given the rise in the number of college students over 30 years of age, there will be a greater demand for continuing education and the faculty and facilities to support it. The demands will challenge educational leaders to plan not just for incremental growth and progress, but a fundamental makeover of institutions. The challenge is not just in increased competition, but in how institutions can be revitalized in preparation for the new era. Schools such as the Apollo Group, Capella Education Company, Sylvan Learning Systems, and Nova Southeastern University are aggressively forcing the hand of traditional schools to rethink strategy, vision and cost. The free market is invading traditional schools, forcing them to compete on costs and service provision. The total annual market is of around 140,000 masters degrees and some 7,000 doctorates. Sylvan is the largest for-profit player in this market. In addition to its Walden University arm, an extensive operation which offers graduate degree programs, Sylvan also serves tens of thousands of students taking non-degree, continuing education. It also operates Cantor and Associates, a unit which provides distance learning hookups to traditional colleges of education. Their Kaplan College of Education and other entrants are poised to launch an education network aimed at midcareer students wanting to switch to the teaching profession.

And notice, virtually none of these new players in educational training offer programs at bachelor level; they are simply too costly to operate. Furthermore, time-honored accreditation processes are no longer as important as they were. Accreditation is still available through the National Council for Accreditation of Teacher Education (NCATE), for those seeking such programs. Grants of Accreditation are based largely on a school's research program and library holdings, factors that will be all but irrelevant to the new wave of mature students.

America has long set the pace for creative and accessible education. There are countless examples of this, but one such is the nontraditional Deep Springs College, in the California High Desert. Few even know of this highly selective and innovative two-year college. Founded in 1917, this all-male school challenges each class with a demanding academic program comprising classical studies, along with cattle and farm labor. Each class has about 15 students and a student-to-faculty ratio of 5:1. Tuition, room and board are provided for each student who qualifies. The program rests upon three fundamental pillars: academics, self-government and labor. It is not a surprise that most graduates go on to excel in some of the world's most respected institutions.

And American women, for the first time ever, have surpassed men in earning doctorates.[72] But the ascent may be specious: the statistics on women show their degree count has stayed about the same (some 13,000 annually), while men's doctorates have been slipping. In particular, doctorates in the physical sciences and engineering have dropped, a fact that concerns many because of national competitiveness issues. Some 19 percent of all doctorates earned by US citizens are awarded to minorities. Of all the doctorates earned in the US by foreigners, the largest shares are from China, followed by South Korea, then India.

Appropriate incentives must be developed for students to graduate early, if not on time. There is a small but growing population of mature students who, for various reasons, want to accelerate through their college years. Part of this is to get into the job market sooner. On the other hand, there is also an increasing number of students who simply want to take their time and are not particularly anxious to leave the academic nest. At the University of Texas at Austin, and typically of other public universities, only 40 percent of their undergraduates now complete their degrees within four years. This is a recent phenomenon that has administrators concerned, as it slows up the efficient throughput of students.

Dual careers and other modern pressures are making for a new faculty workforce: flexible professors.[73] Such arrangements also carry challenges to securing tenure for couples in the same institution or at nearby ones. And there are scheduling issues that need coordination, not to mention worries over career stability for those professors and administrators who must anticipate future needs. Nonetheless, it is catching on. For example, some professors are jointly chairing departments; they are deans multitasking to carry the load more effectively.

---

72. *The Chronicle of Higher Education*, Dec. 12, 2003, p. A10.
73. "Job-Sharing Rises as Professors Seek Flexible Schedules," *The Chronicle of Higher Education*, December 8, 2000, pp. A10-12.

These arrangements can be particularly attractive to small colleges in remote locations, where they can make a real difference in some couples' lives. As an example, there is a married team sharing the presidency at the Institute of Transpersonal Psychology, in Palo Alto, California. And some two decades ago, John B. Willett and Judith D. Singer, full-time education professors at Harvard University, shared a professorship appointment. Later, in separate jobs, they continued to pool their efforts on papers, conference presentations, and even on teaching. Today they are sharing a post once again—the academic deanship of Harvard's Graduate School of Education. They would not have taken the job otherwise.

2. COLLEGE ATHLETICS AND RECREATION

Everyone knows that campus sport is big business, a fact that has many increasingly concerned. College fields, stadiums and arenas are switching from forums offering fitness to high-stakes entertainment venues. The influence of sports on many campuses is breeding a subculture of pre-professional athletes, at the expense of scholarship. Many colleges and universities manage these programs responsibly; some do not, and others are calling for reform.

The US Department of Education has established a Federal commission charged with reexamining Title IX of the Education Amendments of 1972, the law that forbids sex discrimination at institutions receiving Federal funds. The objective, under this Title, is for colleges and universities to provide equal opportunities for participation, proportionally, for all male and female students. But over the years, this Title has been under attack from those who allege that it is an unwritten quota system, used to encourage women to become active in college athletics. These critics say that funds are being siphoned off from men's programs and reallocated to women's that, too often, languish for want of interest. And the finger-pointing continues.

A key question is, just what should be the role of intercollegiate sports in universities? On many campuses its influence is such that athletics is a *cause celebre*. Disturbing cases arise all too frequently of athletes living in special compounds, having special perks and being allowed to take watered-down courses. This new enterprise has become a very big business on too many campuses; so big that many colleges are now rethinking its place in the university.

As a sign of the times, in 2003 Vanderbilt University, an NCAA Division III institution, dismantled its athletics department altogether, and delegated its various components to other departments. Their intent was to keep varsity athletics alive, yet de-emphasize their influence within the university—while still retaining their membership in the NCAA Southeastern Conference. Others, including the Ivy League schools, are wrestling with this same issue.

If athletes can meet the same standards as other students, what is wrong with bringing them to campus and expecting them to perform on an equal basis? There is nothing wrong with that at all, but it often does not work that way. Studies overwhelmingly show that student athletes—and especially those in the high-profile programs of basketball and football—do not measure up academically to their peers. In the case of Ivy schools, the two groups entering college differ by some 165 points on their SAT exams, a substantial margin. Most (81 percent) of those athletes end their academic careers in the bottom third of their class. Those students in other, lower-profile sports such as swimming and wrestling, scored similarly (64 percent of male athletes). Of course, it takes more effort and focus for students to excel at sport as well in class, but rationalizing the situation does not make it right—or fair to other students who do not get special considerations.

The National Collegiate Athletic Association (NCAA) tracks all of its 5,720 teams, in 41 distinct sports, to ascertain which students meet their standard for academic progress, and which do not. In each of the four most popular sports (football, basketball, wrestling and baseball), more than 40 percent of teams failed to meet their own standards. Various groups have now weighed in to fix a situation which is clearly broken. Sanctions have included banning teams from playing in postseason, to withdrawing athletic scholarships. The stakes are high for schools, many of which have long exploited student-athletes.

The NCAA has developed a complex formula, based upon a team's "Academic Progress Rate," which determines whether a team is on track to graduate at least 50 percent of its athletes. To comply and continue competing, each team requires a minimum score of 925 out of 1,000, or 92.5 percent. In the academic year 2003-4 some 1,200 of the 5,720 teams had Academic Progress Rates of 925.

It is useful to compare their academic performance to that of non-athletic students such as musicians, students in government, and legacy students. It turns out that this group achieves in their academic years just about the same as their rank and file colleagues. They are often allowed some leeway in the admissions process.[74]

Scott Cowen, President of Tulane University, and a growing number of his peers are calling for major reform in regards to student athletes. He sees a need for this leadership group to take the reins and reform the dysfunctional intercollegiate sports landscape, along with the increasing abuses thereof. A good start would be to make full public disclosure regarding collegiate student-athletes: courses taken, major fields, Grade Point Averages, and special tutorial perks not afforded to mainstream students.

The NCAA has new guidelines for athletes and their teams,[75] covering:

- New Academic Standards

    Tougher standards for achieving a degree

- Formulas for measuring academic progress

    Annual Academic Progress Ratings

    Percentage of athletes earning degrees (the usual 6-year graduation rate)

    Percentage rate of retention of athletes

    Comparisons with entire student body

- Incentives and Disincentives

---

74. "Reclaiming the Game: College Sports and Educational Values," by William Bowen and Sarah Leven, 2003. "Running Numbers: New Research Reveals that Student Athletes Fall Behind Academically Even at Elite Colleges," *U.S. News & World Report*, Sept. 22, 2003, p. 27.
75. *The Chronicle of Higher Education* April 18, 2003, pp. A43-44.

More money from TV contracts

More coaches

Penalties including expulsions from championships, and loss of scholarships

- Timetable for Adopting the New Rules

The good news is that the NCAA has gotten its message across. During the years 2000 through 2003, the NCAA banned more than 30 Division 1 institutions from competing in certain sports programs. A broad spectrum of sports was included, from rifle, rowing and gymnastics to football and basketball. It is all about economics and recognition of the true purposes and goals of athletics in higher education.

Too often there is an important distinction between students who are recruited as athletes and those who enter as walk-ins—that is, not on coaches' lists at the beginning of the admissions process. Recruited athletes are often given special privileges including free food, lodging and tutoring. Walk-ins generally get involved in athletics as a diversion from academics and just to participate and have fun. Should there be such a distinction?

There are often stark inequities between young scholars and student athletes. Why are athletes supported with scholarships, even though in many cases they may be the most marginal of students? Why are costly tutoring centers and arenas erected to serve mostly this group of students? Why are special dormitories and meals, practice facilities and other perks provided for the sole use of student-athletes? Why are such inequities condoned? These questions lie heavy on state-supported institutions, more so in times of austerity and cutbacks. These questions need to be addressed in the context of the purpose of institutions; they are not just for special interest groups who primarily see the campus as a large sports arena.

Many voices have called for a moratorium on freshmen competing in intercollegiate athletics. There are persuasive reasons for this approach. It would give these young men and women more time to mature, and a better chance of succeeding in their academic programs. Many student-athletes come from marginal high schools, and thus are at a disadvantage when set against mainstream students who are usually better prepared and are not as burdened with practices and games. This is not a new idea; the legendary UCLA basketball coach, John Wooden long advocated and practiced this approach to developing his student-athletes.

These reforms will be hard to enact. College presidents who wish to curb trends that would make collegiate sports even bigger are often overridden by trustees, many of whom are themselves avid sports fans. Organizations like the Association of Governing Boards of Universities and Colleges are working to reform college sports, initially by cutting back on commercialism and ever-growing budgets for big time college sports. James J. Duderstadt, President Emeritus of the University of Michigan (and a scholar-athlete as an undergraduate at Yale, himself), says that if faculty groups put more pressure on their trustees, their presidents will muster the clout to act decisively in reining in college sports. More and more people are questioning why athletes should have their own tutors and special quarters, and why schools succumb to outside pressures to turn a blind eye to athletes receiving unmerited grades just so they may continue their eligibility. The good news is that those voices are now beginning to be heard: Presidents Nannerl O. Keohane, of Duke, and John Hennessy, of Stanford, have spoken out to say that the NCAA faces a "conflict between their dual roles of promoter and governor of intercollegiate athletics."

Afro-Americans comprise about 50 percent of all athletes in US colleges and universities. The average time it takes for Afro-Americans to earn their degrees is about six years. The US Congress and other influential groups accuse coaches of not doing enough to graduate their student-athletes. Some accuse them of exploiting these students by keeping them on the roster even when their grades are trending toward failure. The NCAA has tried to redress this imbalance by prescribing minimum SAT scores for athletes to be eligible for participation in sports (820 on the combined SAT—those with less than a 2.0 average must score at least 1010).

Polls of athletic influence in college sports show that two-thirds of people believe colleges place too much emphasis on athletics. Worse, three-quarters of those polled feel that athletes are not held to the same academic performance standards as other students. Another poll by *The Chronicle of Higher Education*[76] showed that among 21 important goals for colleges, athletics came in last. The preoccupation with men's basketball and football, particularly, is obsessive. Part of the attraction is the "bad boys" who, without the benefit of their coaches' wisdom on priorities and ethics, often sell themselves into obscurity.

It is time for colleges to rein in "big sport" programs and their well-groomed athletes. They must place more emphasis on their other tuition paying students who simply want to use athletic facilities for recreation and fun.

In their book, "Reclaiming the Game: College Sports and Educational Values," William G. Bowen and Sarah A. Levin[77] reveal the inequities among student athletes in America's small, elite colleges. They found that even in these schools, athletics applicants have an advantage in being accepted over the general pool—and especially those most sought after, students who are on coaches' lists. Once enrolled, as a group they tend to be at the bottom of their classes. This may be explained by the demanding schedules of student-athletes, although most students carry various other interests above and beyond their curricular loads. Also, men and women athletes tend to cluster their studies in the business and social sciences areas; rarely in premed, engineering or other more demanding curricula. But on the other hand, it appears that the graduation rates of these athletes are as high as, if not higher, than those of their classmates.

Bowen and Levin have shown that, among Ivy League students, college athletes do less well in academics than their peers with comparable academic credentials. If the compromise is apparent among some of the best prepared students in the US, its effects among less academically prepared college groups can only be imagined. The glorification of these very talented women and men continues, yet they are held to a lesser

---

76. *The Chronicle of Higher Education*, May 2, 2003, p. A17.
77. "Reclaiming the Game: College Sports and Educational Values," by William G. Bowen and Sarah A. Levin

standard. They generally enjoy a significant admissions advantage as compared to those in the general pool of applicants (fourfold in the Ivy League). Interestingly enough, other applicants who bring their credentials in music or theater just do not get such breaks. They simply must be superior performers.

The excesses of collegiate athletics are well known. Administrators must—and will—look carefully at the role of collegiate athletics in their programs. Of course, there are alumni and other groups that will oppose any shift to de-emphasize these privileged programs, especially major sports such as basketball, football, soccer and baseball. There might be some temporary impact on ticket sales and alumni giving, but it seems to be the right thing to do. After all, the primary purpose of student athletic programs is to mold students in learning teamwork and leadership. Winning in school and in life is important, but not at any price.

Having highlighted the excesses of collegiate sports. a good argument can be made that they bring students together, as well as bringing much needed funds to campuses. The big collegiate sports do in fact promote school spirit and a sense of community. Looking at the larger picture, colleges and universities encourage, through their athletics and other programs, other commercial enterprises such as the media, tourism, advertising and marketing that benefit them. It seems, after all, that it would be of benefit to strike an equilibrium which may throttle down big sports' engine, and ensure that minor sports also have their appropriate place.

3. Phony Degrees: New Twists on Education and Measuring Educational Outcomes

One area of mounting concern is the market for phony degrees and bogus diplomas. This is a huge, $600 million market that is doubling every five years. Legitimate home study schools that offer authentic courses have long had to contend with their bogus counterparts. But, with internet access, this cottage industry is growing ever faster, offering graduate degrees, including PhD's, on impressive-looking vellum. So-called administration fees range from $50 to $5,000 for a baccalaureate, masters or doctorate degree.

Is there not a risk of being found out? Yes, but not much. Only 40 percent of US companies regularly and thoroughly verify degrees in their employment processes. These bogus companies, with seemingly prestigious names that sound like actual institutions, advertise in magazines and online, with pitches that seem to be quite legitimate. These degrees are intended to be representative of the scholar's "life and work" experience. This trend is a disservice to America's educational enterprise and the many fine, legitimate nontraditional colleges and universities.

According to Mariah Bear, author of *Bears' Guide to Earning Degrees by Distance Learning*[78], there are some 500 diploma mills and nearly the same number of related Web sites. Moreover, with more legitimate colleges offering online degrees, the environment is ripe for these diploma mills to flourish, because it is increasingly harder to determine whether a degree earned at long distance is actually *bona fide*.

It is fraudulent, but where is the harm? One answer is that the owners of fraudulent certificates are thieves, misrepresenting themselves and stealing trust from others. But the real damage is from people fraudulently presenting themselves as professionals such as doctors and therapists. Statistics confirm that these abuses abound.

In 1992 Congress gave the US Education Department the power to end these scams, and more than 1,500 businesses have since been barred. Yet they still crop up, and continue to poison the well of academic trust and respectability with their phony enterprises.

Sometimes, including fake credentials in a professional portfolio can backfire. In 2003 the Deputy Chief Information Officer of the US Homeland Security Department was caught claiming to hold degrees that turned out to be bogus, including a PhD from one Hamilton University (no connection with Hamilton College in New York). She is no longer a US government employee.

---

78. *Bears' Guide to Earning Degrees by Distance Learning*, Mariah P. Bear, TenSpeed Press, Berkeley, CA.

4. Learning by Degrees

There needs to be more creativity in the quest to inspire students. New ways must be found of combining fact-based and technology-based instruction with individual initiative-based education to enrich the learning process. Self-paced instruction certainly is essential for getting ahead. Higher education is now spilling over into factories and offices. There is investment in corporate universities for lifelong learning. The elements of modern learning are self-study, learning from a professor, and learning from other students.

Internet-based asynchronous education can provide for all three of these elements. The internet has two important and distinguishing attributes for delivering adult education. First, it is an extremely efficient mechanism for distribution of educational materials. Second, it is an effective communication mechanism between learner and professor and among learners themselves. Moreover, there are two distinct learning models: the broadcast, or online publishing, model that is well-suited to training and to non-credit short courses; and the highly interactive model for traditional for-credit courses.

It might surprise some that traditional universities, senior and community colleges are still the dominant providers of for-credit education. In fact, they account for more than 95 percent of the million or so online enrollments. The largest non-profits are the University of Maryland University College, and State University of New York. Among the for-profits, University of Phoenix is the top, though behind Maryland and SUNY in enrollments. The for-profits are struggling. Some will survive and be successful; most will not. In the engineering disciplines, Stanford, Georgia Institute of Technology, University of Washington, and University of Illinois are among the leaders, but all offer only masters degrees.

The challenges facing institutions of higher education, as discussed in this book, are rapidly and fundamentally changing the way we learn. The single word which best defines this new era is complexity. There is a large menu from which to choose in the lifelong quest of learning. That complexity certainly is beneficial to society. But it unsettles many, and imposes upon everyone the responsibility to keep up with the dizzy assortment of choices faced. Therefore there must be better provision and consumption of knowledge. There is a social obligation to support educational enterprises offering better approaches to lifelong learning. Clearly, change is all around. America has fought and won tougher struggles. No doubt, it will win this one as well.

Epilogue

America's system of higher education has served and will continue to serve its people well. However, as with any institution, it must renew itself so that it can provide effectively for future interests and needs. Legacy is rightly honored, yet people must have the vision and the courage to rethink their future. This sometimes means shedding cherished traditions, methods and processes.

They must be replaced with new ones that can bring better access, improved learning tools and pedagogies, convenience, better organizational and cost efficiencies, and stronger accountabilities. Over the centuries there has been little more than small improvements. It is high time that some cherished covenants were let go, and new and even better ways discovered for everyone to learn continually. The courage to do this can, and must, be found. It takes time to remake familiar traditions, but the quest to do so will be successful.